A
NEW
CLIMATE
FOR
STEWARDSHIP

A
NEW
CLIMATE
FOR
STEWARDSHIP

Wallace E. Fisher

Abingdon
Nashville

A NEW CLIMATE FOR STEWARDSHIP

Library of Congress Cataloging in Publication Data

Fisher, Wallace E
A new climate for stewardship.
1. Stewardship, Christian. I. Title.
BV772.F5   248'.6   76-109

ISBN 0-687-27723-X

MANUFACTURED   BY   THE   PARTHENON   PRESS   AT
NASHVILLE, TENNESSEE, UNITED STATES OF AMERICA

*For these Christian teachers who helped to frame
and enlarge my ministry in the Church*

Dunning Idle

Robert Fortenbaugh

Theodore G. Tappert

Elton Trueblood

Contents

Preface

The church needs urgently to become a more responsible steward of God's Word, human and animal life, the earth's resources, and economic goods. Its effectiveness for God—if not its institutional life—depends substantially on its rediscovery of biblical stewardship.

This book is written as a resource for lay people, parish pastors, and church administrators who recognize that crucial need, share the responsibility for meeting it in the congregations throughout the United States and Canada, and earnestly want to do something about it. None of my preceding books on parish life was written under firmer constraint.

My debt for what is written is extensive. I cannot identify all the sources which undergird this presentation, or acknowledge fully my debt to Christian and secular writers who have lighted my way, or express adequately my gratitude to the laity in Trinity Church whose rediscovery and practice of biblical stewardship demonstrates the power of God in and through a congregation which validates the thesis of this study. But the dedication, following acknowledgments and parenthetical notes in the text reflect a measure of my appreciation.

The chapters have benefited from critical exposure in Trinity Church, Lancaster, Pennsylvania. Chapters 1, 2, and 3 and parts of chapters 4 and 5 have been improved by give-and-take discussions in these corners of the Lutheran

Church in America: the Michigan Synod; the Pacific Southwest Synod; the Pacific Northwest Synod; the Capitol District, Upper New York Synod; the Harrisburg and York Districts, Central Pennsylvania Synod; the New Jersey Synod; and in the Nevada-California District of the Lutheran Church-Missouri Synod; an annual conference of evangelism leaders, United Methodist Church, Perkins School of Theology, Southern Methodist University; and the annual convention, National Evangelistic Association, Disciples of Christ. The book was enriched by the hundreds of clergy and lay persons in those meetings who honored me by discussing, affirming, disagreeing with, and debating what I said. Appendix II is a routine compilation of tested ways of doing "dollar" stewardship.

I also want to thank these persons by name. My secretary, Arline S. Fellenbaum, helped at times by our office secretary, Dorothy M. Anne, typed the manuscript. Further thanks are due the generous readers of the manuscript: Larry L. Lehman and B. Penrose Hoover (professional colleagues at Trinity); R. Ray Evelan, Jack R. Hoffman, and Hugo W. Schroeder, Jr. (former professional colleagues at Trinity); and Harvey E. Blomberg, E. Dale Click, Arnold L. Conrad, Robert W. Duke, Lawrence E. Folkemer, Richard G. Frazier, Donald R. Heiges, Arthur J. Henne, Earl R. Henley, Robert P. Hetico, John A. Jarvis, Paul D. Joslyn, David E. Klepper, Jr., John V. Lindholm, W. Robert May, Lawrence R. Recla, Ira A. Sassaman, Carl H. Satre, Jr., Harald S. Sigmar, William R. Snyder, John B. Steinbruck, Clifton M. Weihe, Edward F. Weiskotten, and Arthur M. Yeagy—professional colleagues serving the Church in the United States and in Canada; and these present and former lay members in Trinity Church: our son, Mark Fisher; Cynthia Bolbach, Atty.; Robert P. Desch; Melvin J. Evans; Ruth Grigg Horting; William A. Hutchison, M.D.; Edith C. Mumper; Ann and Elvin Musselman; Jack R. Lesher; Edmund and Ingrid Ruoff; Merle J. Showalter; Debra D. Smith; Ann White, Ph.D.; Kirk White, Esq.; William E. Whitesell, Ph.D.; and Robert H. Witmer, M.D. Their critiques have strengthened the presentation.

Finally, my wife, Margaret Elizabeth, knows better than anyone my debt to her. Nonetheless, I acknowledge gratefully that her critical devotion to God's Word, respect for all life, freedom from "the tyranny of things," and joy in living have enlarged my Christian stewardship.

Lancaster, Pa.   WALLACE E. FISHER

Introduction

THE CHURCH'S NEED TO LEARN
BIBLICAL STEWARDSHIP

*There are times when we can
never meet the future with sufficient
elasticity of mind, especially if we
are locked in the contemporary systems
of thought. . . . Hold to Christ, and for
the rest be totally uncommitted.*
—*Herbert Butterfield*

The church's effective witness during the remainder of
this volcanic century will depend substantially on its
rediscovering and shaping its life to the *biblical* concept of
stewardship. At the same time, it must stand firmly against
a secular-industrial-technological society enmeshed in a
material approach to all life. This complex learning
experience and bold stance in the world cannot wait for the
long called-for "theological reconstruction." Neither will
the *status quo* in society automatically change, adapt, and
grow. If lay and ordained church people in the Protestant
and Catholic churches continue to rely on budgets,
promotional literature, manipulative techniques, shallow
homilies, and, in some quarters, thinly veiled coercive
measures for "doing stewardship," God, weary of a church

that ignores *his* stewardship, may employ other means and other people to accomplish his liberating purpose. (Paul Tillich made this judgment a quarter of a century ago. The course of recent history gives substance to it.) God's love is not gelatinous; it is structured by his righteousness.

Kaleidoscopic events in the 1960s jarred American and Canadian churches into getting more involved in the world. Now, worldwide socioeconomic-political changes in the 1970s are prodding the American church to take up a serious study of biblical stewardship which calls for nothing less than obedience to the whole Word of God. Few congregations anywhere have yet faced up to this difficult task, although the need to do so is crucial. Instead, many appear to be retreating into the neo-conservatism of the 1950s rather than seeking out the living Christ at work in the fragmented world of the 1970s.

God is eager for a new Pentecost. But the church must meet him on the risk-filled frontiers of human need if it wants to experience his renewing power. It cannot, as Pieter M. Bauman observed a half decade ago, "remain splendidly aloof on the top of a pillar in a far-off desert, meditating on 'spiritual things'" *(Can the World Share the Wealth?* [New York: Friendship Press, 1969], p. 6).

Congregational and denominational leaders (ordained and lay) who decide to take biblical stewardship seriously will reexamine personal and parish and denominational priorities in the light of God's revelation and thereafter challenge their members in word and deed to mesh their life-styles with the demands of the gospel. Wherever this process is activated, personal pain and congregational travail will result. Biblical stewardship calls for fundamental changes in the church's outlook and stance on all personal and social fronts. At present, stewardship in the church is preoccupied with raising money to meet budgets oriented primarily to institutionally defined needs and to financing top-heavy bureaucracies. This narrow approach is no longer adequate for an effective witness in the 1970s. The church will learn to exercise God's stewardship in the last quarter of this century, or the church as we know it could become an anachronism in our society by the year 2000.

Any congregation (and denomination) which teaches and acts boldly on biblical stewardship comes into conflict with a society which rapes nature; employs talents and goods for self-interest, corporate interest, and national interest; disdains human life by "body counts" and "triage" thinking; and dismisses out-of-hand the possibility of authentic personhood. But first, a struggle ensues inside the congregation and denomination because members of contemporary society, largely unconverted, people the church rolls. Biblical stewardship calls the church to be obedient to the whole Word of God, to take up Christ's Cross, to meet human needs from the resources of the gospel. Too many members in all congregations are not prepared to pay that price. Nonetheless, a segment of the church, rediscovering that it is "approved by God to be entrusted with the gospel" (I Thess. 2:4), and acting on that discovery, can effect a radical renewal of the church through that remnant. It is Christ who persuades some church members to be servants of the Word rather than servants of self or class or institution. That is costly work for him and for those who affirm his way. Biblical stewardship is a life-style with the Cross at its center. The church must challenge, inform, and persuade its community to embody God's Word in the world if it expects to be a force in society rather than a fungus on it.

The basic purpose of this book is to provide resource material for teaching *biblical* stewardship in the congregation. It focuses on (a) the custodianship of the gospel, (b) the Christian concern for persons, (c) the disciplined care of the earth, and (d) the responsible employment of human resources and economic goods. The book is written for congregations, since biblical stewardship is the primary responsibility of every Christian congregation. Synodical, district, diocesan, and denominational stewardship offices, commissions, and committees may choose to use it for study sessions with representative lay leaders who in turn will lead study groups in single congregations or clusters of congregations. Stewardship is not a parish "activity" to be assigned to a committee; it is the responsibility of each congregation. Biblical stewardship is corporate.

> Stewardship is no optional alternative for the congregation; it is the very stuff of its life together. It embodies or incorporates the community's faith; apart from genuine stewardship there is only a spirituality which pretends to be the result of the Holy Spirit, but is not. The community created by the Spirit can have only one kind of stewardship: corporate stewardship. (T. K. Thompson, ed., *Stewardship in Contemporary Life* [New York: Association Press, 1965], p. 95.)

Some clergy and lay people are ready for a study which seeks to lift the concept of stewardship out of the present congregational-regional-denominational miasma which concentrates on budgets, apportionments, quotas, pledges, proportionate giving, and consultative processes. This book seeks to challenge and enlighten and motivate. It is written for parish pastors, lay persons, church administrators, and seminary students. Its language is non technical; its style is concise. But it is not a simplistic how-to-do-it manual. It is a content-study-discussion course designed to help persons to discern God's Word in the scriptures, to stir congregations to meet human need, and to sustain them in Christ's ministry. Unless congregations can be motivated, enabled, and equipped to do corporate stewardship, Christ's ministry will continue to be maimed, throttled, and aborted. His ministry is not a private undertaking; it is a corporate task. It is the responsibility of the whole congregation.

Because the church—like other social institutions—expresses its life through institutional forms and structures, the methods and mechanics employed to "do stewardship" require critical attention. Broadly defined ways of doing biblical stewardship are presented implicitly and explicitly in chapters 1 to 5. Tested methods for doing "dollar stewardship" (underwriting congregational and church-wide budgets) are cataloged and commented on in Appendix II. Clerical and lay leaders in each congregation will teach biblical stewardship as they judge best in their own situation, but teach it they must or fail God, the church, the world, and themselves.

Christian stewardship is motivated and shaped by a personal-communal commitment to the God who creates and sustains, redeems and liberates, enlightens and nourishes responsive persons. It depends on God's gracious action in creation, redemption, and renewal; and on persons' free yet disciplined response to his continuing deeds. The relationship is close and loving, as a child to a parent, not as a slave to a master or as an employee to an employer. Wayward humans who accept Christ are adopted by God into his family where each person shares fully in his joyous life and in the joy and tragedy of his people. Biblical stewardship is always a family affair, sanctified by the active presence of the Father, Son, and Spirit.

What, then, is *biblical* stewardship? That question is addressed in the first chapter.

Chapter 1

TOWARD A BIBLICAL DESCRIPTION OF STEWARDSHIP

---

*"Would you tell me, please," said Alice,
"which way I ought to go from here?" "That
depends a great deal on where you want to get
to," said the cat.*
    —Lewis Carroll

I am the way, the truth, and the life.
    —Jesus

This news story was sent over the UPI wire service several years ago.

NEW ORLEANS, La.—An attorney researching the title to a piece of property in Louisiana for a loan from the Reconstruction Finance Corporation tracked the records back to 1803. Desiring a record of transactions previous to that date, he consulted a lawyer in New Orleans.

The attorney replied: "Louisiana was purchased by the United States from France in 1803. The title to the land was acquired by France by right of conquest from Spain. The land came into the possession of Spain by right of discovery made in 1492 by a sailor named Christopher Columbus, who had been granted the privilege of seeking a new route to India by Queen Isabella. The good Queen took the precaution of securing the blessing of the Pope of Rome upon the voyage before she sold her jewels to help Columbus. Now the Pope, as you know, is the emissary of Jesus Christ, who is the Son of God, and God, it is commonly accepted, made the world.

"Therefore, I believe it is safe to presume that he also made that part of the United States called Louisiana—and I hope to hell you're satisfied."

That attorney, frustrated by the bureaucratic red tape of the Reconstruction Finance Corporation, got to the source of all life—God. All creation is his. We are not our own, and nothing belongs to us. We are custodians for a brief season. Nothing, especially life itself, belongs to us. And nothing in creation, we are discovering, lasts forever. Many persons on the rolls of American congregations—perhaps a majority—must be taught and motivated to exercise a responsible custodianship of God's manifold gifts if the church is to be a redemptive force in the world. They need to be encouraged to accept God's-deed-in-Christ. It is his Spirit who motivates and enables humans to care responsibly for his Word, themselves, others, and the earth. Christian stewards acknowledge gladly that they are called to share in God's stewardship, which preserves, liberates, and transforms life (John 3:16). Accepting God's promise and his demands, they give back the life they owe, confident that in his "ocean depths its flow may richer, fuller, be." Christian stewards, like Paul sing out, "To me to live is Christ" (Phil. 1:21).

Christian stewardship and the gospel are inseparable. It roots essentially not in programs but in a dynamic relationship with the living God. It is he who defines the inclusive reach of his stewardship, enables willing persons to be little Christs to other human beings, and motivates them to be responsible custodians of his creation and his gospel. Consequently, defining stewardship is as elusive as defining the gospel itself. It simply cannot be done. It is a relationship to be experienced, described, demonstrated. Nonetheless, some attempts at working definitions are worth examing.

Clarence Stoughton, who challenged the United Lutheran Church in America in the 1940s to a larger practice of dollar stewardship, declared, "Stewardship is what I do after I have said: 'I believe.' " That great-hearted definition is too broad to be useful. T. A. Kantonen commends Rendtorff's definition: "Stewardship is that for which I am responsible to God for my fellow-men" (quoted in *A Theology of Stewardship* [Philadelphia: Fortress Press, 1956]). That definition also lacks concreteness and centers on man's response.

Other definitions of stewardship are too narrow to be useful. That is especially evident when the definition identifies stewardship too closely with the gathering of monies for church use. But unbiblical definitions of stewardship flourish in most American congregations and denominational headquarters. During the 1950s, for example, many Protestant church members accepted the institutionally fostered formula that a 50 (current)—50 (benevolence) budget + an every-member canvass + pledging = stewardship.

Several decades ago, the United Stewardship Council in the United States fashioned a definition which satisfied a majority in the church for a season. "Christian stewardship is the practice of systematic and proportionate giving of time, abilities, and material possessions, based upon the conviction that these are trusts from God to be used in his service for the benefit of all mankind in grateful acknowledgment of Christ's redeeming love." The strengths of that definition are still evident. It does not lock Christian stewardship to an annual every-member canvass, is not legalistic, focuses on God's grace, respects human freedom, calls for trusteeship, and suggests servanthood. But as the times tested the church in the turbulent 1960s, that inclusive definition proved to be inadequate. Specifically, lacking corporate character, it failed to provide the church with a stance and style that allowed it to function flexibly and effectively in a radically changing socioeconomic climate.

The world after 1945 changed so radically, and the tempo of change was so rapid, that all social institutions broke stride. Dean Acheson, writing in his memoirs, *Present at the Creation,* described the period 1945 to 1952 in one jarring sentence: "Only slowly did it dawn on us that the whole world structure and order that we had inherited . . . was gone." The church—like the family, public education, and the government—was caught flat-footed by these cataclysmic changes. The nineteenth-century world structure had disintegrated by mid-twentieth century. Consequently, any current effort to describe a stewardship which orients to less than the whole gospel will be limited by cultural hangover.

In the mid-1960s, T. K. Thompson, Executive Director, Department of Stewardship and Benevolence, National Council of Churches, declared that "stewardship, in its Christian sense, is almost impossible to define." What is needed, I think, is not *definition* but *description.* Jesus himself relied on descriptions rather than on definitions. Stephen Spender, the dean of English poets, argues that the poet's task is to describe reality, not to explain or define it. That is the task we take up here. This study attempts to enable lay persons to perceive, describe, and act on the biblical concept of stewardship. A solid place to begin our inquiry is with a broad description of Jesus' life-style and teachings.

Jesus not only valued all life in this world, he was grateful for his own life. He declared repeatedly that his life was given by God. He enjoyed God's creation. Jesus was not a monastic. Except for the year or two when he carried on a public ministry, it appears that he worked at a trade to support himself and his mother. Jesus was neither a mendicant nor a mystic. His appreciation of food and wine prompted his enemies to call him "a wine-bibber and a gluttonous man." Jesus was not an ascetic. Enjoying the whole of life, he wanted everyone to share in the life of the Spirit and to enjoy the fruits of the earth. He urged the rich young ruler to sell everything he possessed, not because he considered earthly goods to be intrinsically bad, but because the rich young ruler valued his possessions more highly than his personhood. When Zacchaeus adopted a life-style oriented to persons rather than to property, Jesus commended him and joined him at dinner. The good samaritan was, Jesus said, the only responsible steward on the Jericho road that day. Jesus spoke five times more often about earthly possessions than about prayer. His person embodied his message, touching real people in a real world. Many American churchmen, hearing Jesus speak about hunger, money, justice, and honesty would complain, "He's not spiritual." But to over-spiritualize either the person or the message of Jesus is to deny not only God's creation but also God himself.

Jesus encouraged his followers to seek first the kingdom of God. He did not call them to poverty, celibacy, fasting, or prayer as ends in themselves. Some followers were poor, and others remained unmarried. Some fasted, and a few elected celibacy while others gave themselves to long seasons of intercessory prayer. With each, however, it was a matter of choice or circumstance. Jesus himself did not define any of those practices as requirements for discipleship. Every petition in the prayer he taught, while set in an eschatological frame of reference, relates concretely to life here and now. His concern for diseased and broken bodies was not less urgent than his concern for disturbed minds and shattered spirits. Jesus saw the kingdom of God as a coming event; he also accepted it as a present reality. Salvation, for him, was a present experience as well as a future promise—mundane as well as eschatological.

The biblical ethic is worked out in human history. It focuses on every facet of human existence in the context of God's whole creation. Neither Jesus' teaching nor his life-style suggests or implies that the material is evil and the spiritual good. He fulfilled and enlarged the Old Testament teaching that God's Spirit lays claim to the whole person. Biblical Christianity is not dualistic; spirit and body are one in the whole person under God. From Genesis to Revelation, the biblical view is consistent: God's Spirit claims human bodies. "One of the most ancient Christian heresies is that Christianity is such a spiritual religion that the abuse and the neglect of the body could be approved. That is why the years of news about the body count in Vietnam was a blasphemy against Christ and a sin against the Holy Spirit who comes in the body or not at all!" (Carl Braaten, *The Whole Counsel of God* [Philadelphia: Fortress Press, 1974], p. 144.) Present-day churchmen need to study Genesis and Deuteronomy, Hosea and Jeremiah before they can appreciate Jesus fully. As the ghost of Marley pursued Scrooge, so the spirit of Marcion haunts contemporary churchmen. We have neglected the Old Testament as part of God's self-revelation; we have forgotten Jesus' own heritage, seeing him divorced from human history. To understand God's-deed-in-Christ we must appreciate the historical context in which he acted in our behalf. God's stewardship calls us to be responsible stewards of his goodness in the context of our history.

God, having created the universe and all life, looked on his creation, declared it good, and took pleasure in it. When humans—his supreme labor of love—turned their backs on him, he did not wash his hands of his wayward creation or bribe them to come home or cajole them into accepting him or frighten them into obedience or coerce them into goodness. He set out instead to reconcile the rebels for his sake and theirs. He revealed his purpose and person, not in the whirlwind and the fire, but in human experience so that he would be understood. From the distant days of Abraham to the tense political era of John the Baptist, the Hebrews caught glimpses of God acting in history. In his own time, he entered into history himself, born of a woman, subject to family disciplines and other human authorities, accepting finally the temporal dominion of the state. "This is the glory of the incarnation, that God is no longer on top of a mountain, no longer making an oracular communication from on high, nor dwelling in unapproachable light. Jesus was the most approachable man of his day but he poured his glory into the most finite form of human flesh and blood." *(Ibid.,* p. 149.) The incarnation also demonstrates what human beings can become when God's Spirit inhabits their bodies; they can embody the mind of Christ here and now. God does not view humans as "souls with ears"; they are not disembodied spirits. Christianity, William Temple was fond of declaring, is the most materialistic of the world religions.

Appropriately, the English origin of the word stewardship is earthy. The steward was the keeper of an enclosure for livestock, the caretaker (ward) of another's property (sty). That Anglo-Saxon word was a translation of the Greek word *oikonomos,* which means, literally, the manager of a house. Both meanings incorporate these concepts according to Thompson: an entrustment, a responsible servant, a final accounting. The *oikonomos* (house manager) and *sty-ward* (keeper of an enclosure) may be compared loosely with the American cowboy who, in the 1870s, supervised cattle drives in the American West, or with the liege knight in the Middle Ages who owed everything to his lord, or with the Judean shepherd who was responsible for the well-being of his flock. The word steward also survives in our contemporary American vocabulary. The Kentucky Derby relies on the chief steward to see that that famous horse race is run properly. The Indianapolis 500 has a chief steward whose significant responsibility is to guarantee an orderly, fair start for the thirty or so racing cars. Gourmet restaurants employ wine stewards, and ships and airlines have stewards and stewardesses who assume responsibility for the well-being of patrons entrusted to their care. In turn, these personal caretakers are answerable to those who own the restaurants, ships, and airlines.

Jesus viewed the steward as the willing custodian of all that God has entrusted to his people for a season: all life, the earth, and the gospel itself. Jesus taught that God holds each steward accountable for the management of what is committed to him, and he demonstrated that radical teaching. The concept of stewardship in the Old Testament called for responsible trusteeship. Jesus accepted that concept only to go far beyond it. He called for personal *initiative* and risk-taking (parable of the talents).

Paul's understanding of stewardship incorporates the main strands of Jesus' teaching. Essentially, Paul saw himself as a steward of the mysteries of God. "Christ appealing by me," is the way he put it. He also viewed the political state as God's steward for the administration of justice and the maintenance of order. Further, he employed the word stewardship to describe God's total plan of salvation. In that, Paul understood Christ precisely. We shall examine this third concept at a later point in this chapter, but first we shall examine more precisely the several meanings of the Greek words for steward and stewardship.

The root word *oikos* meant originally a place of residence. In New Testament Greek (*koine*) this particular word also means a domestic fellowship. It implies in-depth human relationships. It centers on people who share a common roof, a common heritage, a common cause. In Christian context, the word means a common Lord, a common baptism, a common faith. The household is God's; it is his family. Another strand in the Christian meaning of *oikos* suggests that God builds the "house" (II Sam. 7; Ps. 127:1; Heb. 3:4). But he is not regarded as an impersonal technician who simply assembles the building materials. He is perceived as a creative builder who participates actively in and finds personal satisfaction in fashioning each new residential fellowship. Biblical stewardship focuses on God's Spirit motivating humans to get personally involved in God's own work of creation, redemption, sanctification, and social reconstruction. (Luther's explanation of the third article of the Apostles' Creed in *The Small Catechism* illustrates this vigorously.)

For a few years after the Resurrection, worship services in Jerusalem were held in the temple. From the beginning, however, Christian worship services were also conducted in the homes of Christian believers (Acts 5:32). Paul proclaimed the gospel in public assemblies; he also preached from house to house (Acts 20:20). Initially, then, Christian congregations were built on the family. These house congregations, cited frequently in the New Testament (I Cor. 1:16), were gathering places for Christian worship, instruction, fellowship, and corporate witness. For one to be a house manager of these socioreligious units it was required that he oversee his own family household (fellowship) in a style acceptable to God, whose Spirit in turn works through persons to build the house, the family, the fellowship, the congregation. In Paul's view, edification (being built up by God) occurs only within the fellowship of God's people. This is the work of the Holy Spirit who equips the congregation for nurture and service in the world.

These basic meanings of *oikonomia* in the New Testament can be identified: (1) the steward is an overseer, a caretaker, a household manager; he is not an owner (Jesus' parables); (2) the steward is entrusted with the gospel by God himself (Paul's Epistles); and (3) stewardship refers to each Christian's task in God's plan of salvation (Prison Epistles). (I am indebted to Brattgard, *God's Stewards,* pp. 22-188, for this summary statement.)

Luther, steeped in Pauline theology, taught that the Holy Spirit, working through the Word (Christ) *calls* individuals, *gathers* them into Christ's new community (church), *enlightens* them, *nurtures* them, and *motivates* them to *serve* God in the world. Edification in the biblical sense means not only that the individual believer gains new insights into the gospel and matures in the faith; it means equally that the believer is being "built up into the wall of God's house." The individual, maturing in the new community, is an indispensable part of the whole. Any person who hinders God's use of these living stones (new persons) in upbuilding his people violates God's stewardship, his plan of salvation, which is done corporately. It is God's Spirit who enables each Christ-follower to outgrow his natural disposition to use his resources selfishly and to use them freely for God's purposes. This radical change in human nature, accomplished by God's grace, is a basic

strand in biblical stewardship. It testifies to the congregation's proper care of persons. God's stewardship is
corpo ate.

God does not build the house alone. He commits the task
of upbuilding his people to individuals who accept Christ
and acknowledge his Lordship. Christian stewardship is
personal-corporate; it matures in the context of the
congregation. One evidence that a particular congregation
is a royal priesthood is that it channels God's grace to
people in the world. "Christ existing as community"
(Bonhoeffer) is the church. It is the fellowship in which
Christ lives, acts, and has acted in each moment of history
since the Resurrection event. Corporate stewardship is a
distinguishing mark of the authentic Christian congregation. In Thompson's words, "The community created by
the Spirit can have only one kind of stewardship: corporate
stewardship."

We observed above that Paul also viewed stewardship as
God's plan of salvation. In his letter to the congregation at
Colossae, he specifically identified stewardship as God's
plan to save the world: "Now I rejoice in my sufferings for
your sake, and in my flesh I complete what is lacking in
Christ's afflictions for the sake of his body, that is, the
church, of which I became a minister according to the
divine office which was given to me for you, to make the
Word of God fully known, the mystery hidden for ages and
generations but now made manifest to his saints. To them
God chose to make known how great among the Gentile
are the riches of the glory of this mystery, which is Christ in
you." (Col. 1:24-27.)

Paul's meaning comes into clear focus when we recall
that the first-century Greco-Roman world was inundated
by the mystery religions which claimed to reveal the secrets
of human life and of the universe. Their popular appeal

forced the older Greek cults to adopt their style and stance. In Paul's day, the masses, not knowing whom to believe or what to believe, tried first one cult and then another. Plutarch (Greek biographer and philosopher, A.D. 46-129) got involved in several different mystery religions without finding satisfaction in any one of them (see Brattgard, *God's Stewards,* for a fuller account). Educated people were inclined to consider all religions equally true and equally false. It was in this eclectic religious climate that Paul framed his famous address on Mars Hill to the men of Athens (Acts 17:16-34).

Paul, alert to the cultural situation and remembering his own spiritual frustration before Christ freed him, declared boldly that the true mystery-secret had been revealed to him in the person of Christ, who in turn had commissioned him and other Christian disciples to share this true mystery with the world. He announced to the congregation at Corinth: "Yet I do speak wisdom to those who are spiritually mature. But it is not the wisdom that belongs to this world, or to the powers that rule this world—powers that are losing their power. The wisdom I speak is God's secret wisdom, hidden from men, which God had already chosen for our glory, even before the world was made. None of the rulers of this world knew this wisdom. If they had known it, they would not have nailed the Lord of glory to the cross." (I Cor. 2:6-8 GNMM.) Paul argued that the secret which God had revealed in the Crucifixion-Resurrection event was the full disclosure of God's own stewardship: his personal plan for the redemption, establishment, and proper management of his divine-human household. This God-centered view of stewardship is also found throughout Paul's letters, but especially in Ephesians and Colossians.

Paul's view is on this order. God's stewardship is his

personal plan for the redemption of the world through his Son's birth as a human, his life, his teachings, his death, his resurrection, his victorious presence in the church. God incarnate—the Risen Christ—always acts in and through his co-laborers, the church, to reclaim God's world. This divine-human fellowship is the only community on earth that has been entrusted with the true mysteries of God. The head of this fellowship is Christ, God's Chief Steward, who does his Father's will and enables his followers to share in that redemptive work. The four Evangelists are in agreement with Paul. They testify to Jesus' absolute obedience to God's will. They emphasize that Christ's call to his followers is the call to obedience to his way. The essence of Christian stewardship, then, is to do God's will with Christ as guide and strength. That is every Christian's true vocation. The community of persons called and empowered to take up this task is Christ's church. The gospel, the church, and God's stewardship are inextricably bound together.

Jesus' stewardship of God's mysteries is the living model for his followers. He allowed nothing to deter him from going where God asked him to go and doing what God wanted him to do. When Peter tried to dissuade his friend from going to Jerusalem—God's clear course—Jesus recalled his central mission: "The Son of man came not to be served but to serve, and to give his life as a ransom for many" (Mark 10:45). Jesus committed himself to God's plan of salvation; it was his stewardship. Consequently, it is the church's only proper stewardship if it elects to be true to Christ.

It should be noted that the words steward and stewardship in Jesus' speech, though infrequent, occur mostly in Luke. But the *concept* of stewardship as the doing of God's will, the responsible management of God's family affairs is a dominant strand in his teaching: the talents and pounds (Matt. 25:14-30; Luke 19:11-28); the wicked steward (Luke 16:1-9); the unprofitable servants (Luke 17:7-10); the unmerciful servant (Matt. 18:23-25); the laborers in the vineyard (Matt 20:1-16); the unlike sons (Matt. 21:23-28); the tribute money (Mark 12:12-17; Matt. 20). In these parables the Old Testament views of steward and steward-ship receive a new look in Jesus' teaching. It goes something like this: God not only appoints trustees—overseers, stewards—who are responsible to him; he involves himself in their work. Jesus calls him Abba—Father (literally, *Daddy*). The Galilean declared that he was not a hireling; he was the only Son and the only heir. Because Christ accepts his followers as brothers and sisters—co-heirs—Christian stewards live in the father-child relationship. The house where stewardship takes place is the Father's house. Christian stewardship is a *family* affair. No task on earth is more dignified, liberating, or fulfilling than the work which enable us to share in God's plan to save the world. That is his stewardship. It is the church's task to exercise God's stewardship.

Jesus' side-by-side parables of the prodigal son and the older brother (Luke 15:11-26) underscore this truth. The action in both parables revolves around the two sons, but the central figure is the father. Without the father, the sons would not have existed. Without the father, there would have been no inheritance for the prodigal son to squander, no fields for the older brother to till. Without the father, there would have been no home for the prodigal to remember, to return to, to be accepted in. Without the father's love and forgiveness and acceptance, there would have been no fresh beginning for the prodigal. Without the father's willingness to share his possessions, his home, and his person with both sons, the older brother's hard work would have been in fact the burden he complained of rather than the liberation that it offered him.

Christian stewardship recognizes and accepts the reality that our human existence and personal resources and fields of labor and witness, the earth's resources, and above all, the gospel itself depend on God's creative, sustaining, redemptive work. Stewardship is every Christian's true vocation. Stewardship is every congregation's primary responsibility.

We shall examine this more fully in chapters 2 through 5.

Chapter 2

THE CUSTODIANSHIP OF THE GOSPEL, THE CARE OF PERSONS, AND THE CARE OF THE EARTH

---

*O God, who in Thy loving kindness dost
both begin and finish all good things; grant
that as we glory in the beginnings of Thy
grace, so we may rejoice in its completion;
through Jesus Christ our Lord. Amen.*
—Leonine Sacramentary

In the first chapter, we attempted to identify and describe some biblical meanings of stewardship. In this chapter and the next we shall endeavor to present *biblical* stewardship in the context of these historical realities: the church's custodianship of the gospel, the church's concern for persons, the church's teachings on the care of the earth.

The Custodianship of the Gospel

The church's primary service to God and the world is its responsible stewardship of biblical truth—God's Word. That is where biblical stewardship begins. How the church discerns the Word of God couched in the words of human beings, how it teaches the relationship between the Word and the Bible, how it understands revelation and history, and how it applies biblical truth in concrete situations determine whether its custodianship of the gospel is responsible or not.

At present, however, there are wide differences on these issues in the grass roots church. Certain conservative Christians name Billy Graham, Harold Lindsay, and Oral Roberts as faithful custodians of biblical truth. Main-line Protestants look to Roger Shinn, Paul Lehman, and Joseph Fletcher as responsible stewards of the mysteries of God without feeling any constraint to agree with them fully. In Catholic circles, Hans Küng and the Berrigans exercise a custodianship of biblical truth which is rejected or ignored by the majority of Catholic priests and bishops. Radical differences in biblical interpretation and witness also appear among Christian lay people. William Stringfellow and Keith Miller are poles apart in their Christian approach to life. Catholic writer Dorothy Day and Protestant faith healer Kathryn Kuhlman live in different intellectual worlds. The current differences in biblical interpretation, understanding, and application which beset main-line Protestant clergy and laity are chasmic.

W. A. Visser t'Hooft, while serving as General Secretary of the World Council of Churches, declared that the renewal of the church "is based on hearing anew the Word of God as it comes to us in the Bible." True! Yet discerning the Word in human language poses serious problems in all churches, and acting on it in concrete situations stirs controversy in every congregation. Who are the responsible stewards of God's Word? To determine that we must first determine how the church understands this highly charged phrase, "the Word of God." Paul Tillich has differentiated a half dozen meanings of the phrase in Christian theology.

Main-line Protestant churches agree substantially that the Word of God is the good news of God's saving work in Christ. They accept it as the message about the essential nature and purpose of God's dynamic, saving activity, initiated at Creation and revealed progressively at his pace (comprehended unevenly and communicated substantively by humans) through myth, legend, drama, historical events, historical persons (Amos, Hosea, John the Baptist), and preeminently in the historical person of Jesus of Nazareth. Scripture is the inspired record of human witness to God's saving activity in history. Main-line Protestant denominations also agree that the key to interpreting *all* scripture is Christ—his person and his teaching. That was Luther's view: "If the scriptures themselves, as a whole, claim to be the Word of God, they can be this only if they are, as a whole, interpreted in terms of Christ . . . . Christ is Lord of the scriptures." The biblical account of God's saving activity is more than a report. The Christ event, rooted in an identifiable moment of history, is not bound by history.

But, while all Protestants agree that the scriptures are the church's primary authority in all matters of faith and practice, the authority of the scriptures has in fact become blurred for all Protestants and undermined for most. At the grass roots, church members face a triple task: releasing the dead hand of denominational or sectarian traditions which are cultural rather than biblical, achieving substantive agreement on the relationship between the scriptures and the Word of God, and resolving conflicting interpretations of the scriptures' witness to God's mighty deeds. All three tasks relate integrally to defining and demonstrating the nature and significance of biblical authority. What prevails now in all denominational and sectarian congregations is confusion roughly organized.

In the turbulent aftermath of the Reformation period, separate groups (Calvinists, Lutherans, Anabaptists), accepted the scriptures as their rule of faith, and developed traditions peculiar to their own historical experience (polity, liturgy, dogma, ethics). The varied and often competing Protestant traditions in America root in (a) differing European orgins, (b) the American frontier experience, (c) local mores, and (d) the sharp differences within the church over the *authority* of the scriptures in faith and in concrete life situations.

Biblical scholarship exists to help the church to preach and teach "the whole counsel of God." If it is to aid in this task it must find a solid place in the congregation's teaching ministry. The pulpit (catechetical sermons), church school classes (content and methodology), and small study groups (dialogue and application) must be employed for this purpose so that lay persons can be equipped to discern God's Word in the language of the persons who wrote the texts. Biblical scholarship respects no denominational or sectarian tradition. It seeks to discern the divine Word in human words. This aspect of stewardship must be cultivated in the congregations. Each congregation should be for its members a little seminary.

One evidence that a congregation is a responsible custodian of God's Word is its willingness to accept this teaching responsibility and act on it. The pastor is the chief teacher, but he is not the only teacher. The elected lay leaders' primary responsibility is not economic but biblical and theological. Their first responsibility is to see that the Word of God is rightly preached and taught by the "professional(s)" *and* the appointed lay teachers and that the whole congregation teaches the Word responsibly in the community. Until this happens in local congregations, Jesus may be imprisoned in a book, obscured by the mists of value judgments, "the man nobody knows." Lay people must be challenged, motivated, and equipped to explore the fundamentals of the Faith, if they are to understand and accept the fundamental article in the Faith: God was in Christ reconciling the world unto himself. Critical scholarship enables the church to identify and understand the various historical contexts in which God's mighty deeds were accomplished, since many were the forms and ways in which God spoke to our fathers. It helps one to establish the original meaning of a text. This is an urgent need in the church today.

The critical custodianship of the Word guards against the limitations inherent in demythologization and symbolism. It guards against literalism and moralism. It also provides a solid perspective for evaluating and appreciating "charismatic gifts." Extensive demythologization of the New Testament loses Christ and his message in the mists of value judgments. Literalism imprisons Christ in a book, thus devaluing his message. Charismatic gifts, accepted uncritically, obscure Christ. The Bible must be allowed to speak its sovereign message to a needy world. That is elemental to the church's responsible stewardship of God's Word.

Christians believe in the Bible because of Christ. Correlatively, they believe in Christ because of the inspired biblical record. The faith of the church rests on both views. Scripture is the church's primary authority, but that authority is weakened unless Christ's Lordship over the scriptures is recognized, acknowledged, and acted on. This is crucial to interpreting scripture reliably. A solid custodianship of the gospel also sees to it that Jesus, God the Redeemer, is not separated from the whole biblical faith:

God the Creator of the human family and the natural world and the God of history (measures of social justice now and full victory in the coming of his kingdom). This holistic view rescues scripture from the murky swamps of existentialism and liberates it from the dark prison of literalism. It does so because it accepts and works with history and faith, facts and values. This contextual view—historical and existential, objective and subjective—guides the church in exercising a responsible stewardship of God's whole Word.

When any congregation acknowledges that the Bible is the substantively inspired human record of God's progressive self-revelation—and interprets the *whole* record in the light of Christ's teaching, life, death, and resurrection—that congregation can face the historical fact that the Old Testament writers borrowed heavily from other ancient religions. That congregation can recognize that myth is employed in the Old Testament to communicate God's cosmic deed (Creation) and man's irrational choice (the Fall). The congregation can accept legend (David and Goliath) and drama (Jonah and Job) and apocalyptic discourse (Daniel and Revelation) as human media through which God speaks. That congregation can recognize that the prophetic message in the Old Testament, firm in its promise of Christ, is valued primarily not as an oracular thrust into a "future" we now know, but essentially as the prophetic word in the onrushing witness to God's unbroken presence in judgment and mercy in human experience which came to full expression in Jesus of Nazareth and continues in history through the fellowship of people who accept and serve the Living Christ in current situations. The sovereign, righteous, law-giving God of the Israelites is the patient, merciful, suffering servant (Isaiah 53) whom the Christian church knows, loves, serves, and proclaims as the Resurrection Christ. That is the scriptures' central testimony: God was in Christ reconciling the world to himself; be reconciled to him. The Incarnation and the Resurrection are the focal points in the scriptures' witness to God's liberating deeds in history. Christ is the absolute authority for interpreting all scripture: "You have heard it said in the past . . . , but I say to you . . ."

This dynamic stewardship of God's Word orients not only to God's self-revelation in the past (the Bible), but also to his continuing revelation in contemporary history (the Resurrection Christ). To ignore or down-play either activity is to rob scripture and Christ of their depth dimensions. Scripture is human experience with God at the center of it. God acted as he did in Old Testament days because he would, in the fullness of time, do what he did in Christ. Luther's suggestion that we should begin with the sayings of Jesus makes sense: "Scripture begins tenderly and leads us to Christ as a man, then to the Lord over all creatures, and then to God." But he does not say that Jesus' teachings are the whole Word of God. The church accepts scripture as the substantively inspired witness to God's progressive self-revelation and works of liberation.

A proper custodianship of the Word also recognizes that God's self-revelation is not an idea to be possessed. It is the past, present, and future activity of God to be recognized, acknowledged, and anticipated. Anders Nygren has said that "the Bible is the message about this continuing action. But this message is itself an action of God." When it is proclaimed and responded to, therefore, God continues and completes his action in persons. The message of Christ, Luther observed, is not "an old song about an event that happened 1500 years ago. . . . It is a gift and bestowing that endures forever." The Christ event, rooted in history, is not bound by history.

The church's responsible stewardship of God's Word is strengthened or weakened as each congregation teaches (or fails to teach) people how to discern the Word in the human language of the Bible and to act on it in the world. The unity between the Old and the New Covenants is inherent in God's revelation. The key to understanding both covenants is Christ, the Lord of the scriptures.

One firm strand, then, in the church's proper custodianship of the Word requires each congregation to teach and practice the *critical* as well as the *devotional* use of the Bible, to foster solid biblical study, to engage in serious God-talk, and to fashion risk-taking ministries. The scriptures are like the flesh and blood in which Christ came into history as a man. They are the inspired record of God's self-revelation inside human experience. If that record had not been committed to writing, there would be no faith in God through Christ today, and the life of Jesus would be a forgotten event—or a dimly remembered event—in the world's history.

The church exercises a responsible stewardship of the gospel when congregations teach their members how to discern the Word of God in the human language of the Bible. The church is true to its stewardship of the mysteries of God when, at its grass roots, it proclaims and teaches that Word and from its resources motivates its constituency to let Christ inhabit their persons and through them serve others in the world. This solid custodianship of the Word is every congregation's cornerstone in its Christian care of persons.

The Church's Care of Persons

God entrusted his message to the community of Christ-followers, the church. Biblical stewardship is corporate. Christian believers are not loners, they are members of a fellowship. Each believer is a living stone in the house that God is building. The congregation's responsible care of persons *in* its fellowship and its concern for those *outside* its fellowship are primary strands in biblical stewardship. (Recently, I presented an extensive description of the caring congregation in my book *Because We Have Good News* [Nashville: Abingdon Press, 1974]. See especially chapter 3, "The Integrity of the Evangelizing Congregation.")

The Christian care of persons finds its dynamic in and takes its content from God's Word. Since we have examined that cornerstone, since we shall examine Christian stewardship of the self in chapter 3, and since the church's care of persons is dealt with implicitly in chapters 3 and 5, we shall simply identify several areas where the local congregation's responsibility for persons can be examined with a degree of objectivity.

The first step in caring for persons *in* the congregation and for nonmembers *through* the congregation, we observed, is to persuade and enable the former to discern, study, and incarnate the living Word of God; to persuade the latter to take an active place in Christ's church; and to encourage both to strive for a just society for the sake of God and humanity. Personal evangelism and social action are essential strands in every congregation's proper stewardship. Obviously, this course is not being followed totally in any single congregation anywhere, and it is scarcely being followed in most congregations everywhere. Almost a hundred years after solid biblical scholarship had equipped the clergy in main-line Protestant churches to discern more clearly the divine Word in human words, thousands of churches are being ministered to today by men and women who, though trained in biblical criticism, have not taught—or have not been allowed to teach—the laity how to use it. Until the congregation equips its members to discern the Word of God in the language of the authors of the texts, its evangelism will not be indigenous nor its social action integral to its life. Both require that the congregation be grounded in and nurtured from the Word of God.

Another area where main-line Protestant congregations violate biblical stewardship is defined by their ingrained disposition and culturally conditioned practice of valuing property above persons. Most churches, their paying ranks recruited mainly from middle-income and upper-income families, are not aggressive in attacking poverty and other grave injustices in our urban-technological society. Most middle-class church members who are critical of the federal welfare program for millions of ill-nourished, ill-clad, and ill-housed Americans support corporate welfare gladly. In the 1960s it was not the white Christian church—except for a minority of its members—but poor people, white and black, and youth who clamored for a reordering of priorities in military spending. A middle-class church is still speaking softly, indeed barely speaking at all, at the grass roots on this far-reaching human issue.

The church in America, Protestant and Catholic, lags behind some humanists, agnostics, atheists, and a minority of its own members who argue cogently that the American government, under the Bill of Rights, should be held as accountable for protecting human rights as for protecting property rights. Most middle-class church members in the sixties, reflecting John Locke's views on property, were more concerned about the destruction of property in Watts, Newark, Detroit, Washington, Chicago, and Kent State and Jackson State than they were about the loss of human life in those places or about the moral failures of the body politic which spawned those riots. The majority of American church members—at least before the Tet offensive—accepted, endorsed, or tolerated the Vietnam War with its doctrine of search and kill, napalming the countryside, destroying villages to save them, and body counts. Biblical stewardship calls for the care of persons outside as well as inside the institutional church. Most professing Christians fall far short of following him who said, "I am come to seek and to save those who are lost."

Three decades after the nuclear holocaust in Hiroshima and Nagasaki, major ecclesiastical groupings, except for the several "peace churches" (Mennonite, Brethren, Quaker) and clusters of main-line Protestant church members here and there, have scarcely stirred themselves to think seriously about the socioeconomic-humane implications of technological warfare. The concept of the "just war"—forged in ancient times and thereafter lodged in the thinking of the Reformers—was obliterated by the two mushroom clouds over Japan in August, 1945. Yet the church has not addressed this awesome reality in any concerted and serious fashion.

Biblical stewardship also calls the institutional church to establish broad standards of church membership which encourage commitment and demonstrate integrity in persuading persons to join a particular congregation, to provide solid instruction in the faith for all members and to enable them to be Christ-bearers in the world. That is tangible evidence that a congregation cares for persons. It is a strand in its exercise of biblical stewardship.

A congregation's effective care of persons inside its fellowship and concern for persons outside its fellowship are also measured by the biblical content of its formal preaching and teaching. Unless these primary functions of ministry communicate the living Word which shatters the ego, levels and widens the inner life, underscores God's design for living responsibly in his world by caring for perso s and building the new life in Christ, the congregation can be charged with poor stewardship in proclaiming and teaching the gospel. When any congregation allows its preaching-teaching ministry to orient exclusively to any *single* thrust—peace of mind, social action, Bible-reading as a self-fulfilling exercise, winning new members as an end in itself, or tithing as a mark of righteousness—that congregation is not exercising God's stewardship.

To care responsibly for someone or something requires more than a "feeling" for that person or the glib assurance, "We care." To care for another human being is to provide for his whole person, to attend to his full needs—physical and spiritual, and to offer Christ's friendship. This requires commitment, compassion, and competence. Compassion without competence and commitment is ineffectual. Commitment without competence and compassion is cold. Competence without compassion and commitment is sterile.

Employing these and other tests, most members can determine reasonably well whether their congregation really cares for persons or only claims to care for them. In chapters 3 and 5 we shall examine the congregation's care of persons, part of its proper stewardship, in larger detail. Next, we shall consider the church's teachings on the proper care of the earth, which is an inseparable part of its care of persons.

The Care of the Earth

To care for God's Word is to care for persons. To care for both is to care for the earth. Ecological concern is an elemental strand in biblical stewardship. America, like other industrial-technological societies, has been forced to its present moment of truth by the earth's deteriorating environment and dwindling resources. This planet's premature death is being predicted by sober-headed scientists. Ecology is not, as some critics charge, a white, middle-class cop-out from facing other pressing social issues. It is, in one sense, the crucial social issue affecting all other issues. Church members in the West, no less than non-church persons, have shared directly and indirectly in plundering the earth. They must admit, as Pogo did, "We have met the enemy, and they is us." The "crisis in Eden" is on everyone's doorstep.

This worldwide problem roots first in the inconstancies of human nature. All humans, in and outside the church, have a thin sense of being selfish, assume readily they are critical-minded, rarely examine their own motives in depth. Comfort more than character, convenience more than conscience dictate current life-styles in the West. Linked with these human disabilities which produce a complex of cause and effect is the present disillusionment with democratic ideals and processes in the United States. The American Dream was nurtured in part by the conviction that the political machinery in our republican form of government constituted the best means for realizing equal justice in a stable social order. Democracy was a noble experiment to most Americans; it was a holy experiment to some. Most Americans endorsed the Jeffersonian premise that all citizens could and should participate not only in forming the nation's values but in making governmental decisions as well. But that belief and the representative legislative process became increasingly difficult to maintain and employ in an emerging industrial-technological society which had framed its political philosophy and fashioned its republican form of government when it was an agrarian society. Executive power grew steadily during the Great Depression, World War II, the Cold War, the competition in nuclear armaments, the space flights, the Great Society, the Vietnam War, and Watergate. The citizenry's rising disillusionment with big government was in the making for decades.

While the CIA's abortive invasion of Cuba and the credibility gap over Vietnam and Watergate were overpowering events which effected that disillusionment, there were many confidence-sapping events from 1945 to 1965. Recall one: the uphill fight waged by the pioneers of ecological reform. Rachel Carson, an early champion, engaged in research on the debilitating effect of insecticides on the environment in the 1950s. The attacks on her work from chemical corporations and other threatened industries and businesses and from the Department of Agriculture were harsh. (See Paul Brooks, *The House of Life* [Greenwich, Conn: Fawcett, 1972], chapters 17–20.) One major chemical trade magazine, commenting on Carson's *Silent Spring* (1962), crassly placed profits above persons: "Industry can take heart from the fact that the main impact of the book will occur in the late fall or winter seasons when consumers are not normally active users of insecticides. . . . It is fair to hope that by March or April, *Silent Spring* no longer will be an interesting conversational subject." (Reported in *ibid.*)

Nonetheless, Ms. Carson's book had an escalating impact on citizens in all nations, and on their governments, including her own. The publication of the President's Science Advisory Committee Report (1963), supporting many of Ms. Carson's conclusions, marked a turning point in the controversy aroused by her book. Since 1963, slow but definite action has been taken to protect the citizen-consumer against indiscriminate uses of insecticides. DDT, an insecticide viewed as potentially carcinogenic, had been largely phased out by January, 1971. Carson's research also had a solid impact on other industrial nations. The British government, for example, was immediately impressed. Lord Shackelton, speaking in the House of Lords in support of Carson's thesis, made his point humorously— even as he betrayed his own racism—with a story of the cannibal chief in Polynesia who no longer allowed his tribe to eat Americans because "their fat is contaminated with chlorinated hydrocarbons!" *(Ibid.,* p. 269.) Pioneers like Rachel Carson, Margaret Mead, Ralph Nader, and Noel Mostert have helped to heighten public consciousness of current environmental hazards.

The ecological problem is psychological and political. It is also techno-economic and theological. The following excerpts from an article by an Associated Press writer reporting the first recorded air pollution disaster three decades ago in Donora, a little mill town in western Pennsylvania, provide perspective on the problem.

> For most of the 12,000 residents on that Wednesday, Oct. 27, 1948, thoughts were elsewhere. . . .
> Elections were a week away. The baseball season had been over for three weeks and the town's native son, Stan Musial of the St. Louis Cardinals, had had another fantastic season, leading the league in batting with a .376 average.
> The U.S. Weather Bureau reported dispassionately that a high-pressure system had created a temperature inversion— cold, dense air was trapped in the valley beneath a layer of warm air.
> It also trapped the tons of soot, fumes, and smoke that poured out of the stacks of a steel mill and zinc works, from chimneys, auto exhausts, trains, and passing boats.
> The statistics: twenty dead; 5,910 persons, or 42.7 percent of those living in the area, were sickened, including 1,440 who were severely ill. . . .
> It said the pollutants came from the mills, 2,300 other

buildings that burned coal or oil for heat, an average of 22 boats a day that passed on the river, 18 freight trains, and six passenger trains, 10 switch engines and an estimated 3,000 automobiles that burned an estimated 26,000 pounds of fuel a day. (Greensburg, Pa. *Tribune-Review,* April 16, 1970.)

The Donora millworkers had grown accustomed to polluted air in the decades before 1948. They accepted it as their fathers before them had accepted it, because smoke-filled skies in the valley meant full lunch pails. In spite of the significant forward strides made to curtail air pollution in the Pittsburgh area and other industrial areas, and in spite of emission controls that have been legislated, apathetic attitudes persist in most air-polluted industrial areas in 1976.

A few days before Earth Day 1970, smog darkened the skies over Gary, Indiana, as it had for decades. A laborer in a steel mill told an investigative reporter that day, "Hell, it means five-fifty an hour to me." In late 1974, a federal district court fined United States Steel $2,300 a day until the remaining open hearths they operated in Gary were replaced. The corporation promptly closed its open-hearth section. But many industrial plants, particularly older ones, as in the paper industry, have little choice except to close down completely because the cost of controlling emissions and effluents is beyond their resources.

Ecological reform and economic stability are more difficult to balance in an urban-technological society than concerned citizens realize. In fact, the price tag on far-reaching reforms is more within reach economically than psychologically. Essentially, a simpler life-style is required. That will not come easy to Americans and western Europeans who are accustomed to creature comfort and affluence. When a majority of Americans realize that effective action to recover and protect their natural environment will reduce their creature comforts, cost hundreds of billions of dollars, and restrict "free enterprise" as they define it presently, many will falter in pressing for ecological reforms. (Some responsible economists estimated in the 1960s that it would cost $120 billion a year to keep environmental deterioration gradual in our industrial society. The cost in 1976 might be $200 billion or more. Others refute that claim.) While millions of people are starving and demographers are calling for zero population growth in the world before the year 2000, the concept of planned parenthood has scarcely taken hold in Asian, African, and Latin American countries. At present, the population of India is increasing annually by 11,500,000 persons. In March, 1975, Premier Gandhi was chiding Western ecologists concerned over population control for getting into God's bailwick. But responsible stewardship of the earth's resources is a worldwide problem. Ignorance, apathy, and selfishness hinder people everywhere in the world in opting for the quality of life because it has high economic, psychological, and cultural price tags attached to it. Self-discipline is rare in all societies, because it is rare in individuals.

Historical records demonstrate that London had a smog problem from burning soft coal in its crowded wooden houses as far back as 1285 (Lynn White, Jr., "The Historical Roots of Our Ecological Crisis," *The Environmental Handbook,* ed. Garrett De Bell [New York: Ballantine Books, 1970], p. 14). But soft coal provided a steadier heat than logs; it was more convenient and more comfortable. Open pit mining scars the landscape and pollutes nearby streams, but it provides fuel for an energy dependent economy. Human nature resists changes which reduce creature comforts, lay siege to pocketbooks, and threaten insecure egos. A half decade ago, John D.

Withers, commenting on the rising urgency for ecological reform, lamented, "We seem unable to manage change; we appear only to react to change." This lack of desire to change—and the will to persevere in effecting change—are built-in human deterrents to ecological reform. The enormousness of the problem in a technological society, when linked with the ego faults in human nature, militates against radical changes in private and public attitudes, educational programs, industrial procedures, and state and federal laws. Noel Mostert, in his *Supership*—a fascinating, frightening report on the 200,000- and 300,000-ton oil tankers (New York:Knopf, 1974)—proves the awesome threat that these behemoths pose to safety at sea and to our environment. But without oil, the industrial nations cannot survive. It is not likely, therefore—in spite of these dangers—that the oil companies will return voluntarily to smaller, safer tankers since the Suez Canal has been reopened. The ecological problem is complicated by human nature.

If the church takes biblical stewardship seriously and jumps into this ambiguous problem with both feet, it will get bloodied. Many already charge angrily that Judeo-Christian teaching is largely responsible for the environmental crisis. They claim that the anthropocentric view in the Bible (man's God-given dominion over nature) encouraged him to exploit nature uncritically. But these critics do not recognize that the Bible presents another view, which presents God, not man, at the center of creation. This theocentric version (Gen. 1:29) holds that human beings are called to be stewards, custodians of God's creation; humans were *not* given a blank check on the environmental bank. Arguing this theocentric view, C. F. D. Moule, in his *Man and Nature in the New Testament* (Philadelphia: Fortress Press, 1967), states that man is "meant to have dominion over it [earth] and use it . . . but only for God's sake, only like Adam in paradise, cultivating it for the Lord. As soon as he [man] . . . reaches out to take the fruit which is forbidden by the Lord, instantly the ecological balance is upset and nature begins to groan."

Nonetheless, some critical minds in this generation insist that the responsibility for raping the earth stems from Judeo-Christian teaching. Professor Withers himself declared a decade ago that "the historical roots of our ecological crisis are deep in the Judeo-Christian tradition." He argued that "western man has been imbued with a perception of nature in which air, land, and water are exploitable because they are assumed to have been created to serve his purpose. This tradition tells us that man is for the glory of God, but I would submit that the same is true for all creations of the Creator."

Withers' judgment was influenced by an article, "The Historical Roots of Our Ecological Crisis," which was published in 1967 by Lynn White, Jr., distinguished professor of history at Stanford University. White's article appeared first in the March, 1967, issue of *Science*. He has expressed amazement at the wide response it gained. But he did link the environmental crisis to Judeo-Christian teaching. Because White's thesis has had an unusually wide impact on the intellectual community, I shall present his central argument. White argues that the current rape of the environment is a result not only of the industrial-technological revolution and the natural human disposition to serve one's own immediate interests, but also of the Judeo-Christian teaching that God, having created man, gave him dominion over all natural life (except human life), prodded him to subdue the earth, and commanded him to multiply. According to Professor White, this anthropocentric position—in contrast to ancient paganism and current world religions—fostered a dualism in man and nature which encouraged people in Western civilization to exploit nature for their own selfish purposes. He argues that this attitude toward the natural environment must be recognized and altered radically if an effective ecology is to be developed. White's thesis is open to criticism on biblical and historical grounds.

Frederick Elder placed this controversial issue in biblical perspective in his careful study, *Crisis in Eden* (Nashville: Abingdon Press, 1970). There he discusses first the anthropocentrism in the "popular" account in Genesis. Next, he points out that decades ago biblical scholars identified two different creation stories written from two separate sources, J and P. In the J source, man is indeed dominant. But the P source places God, not man, at the center of life. In the second account (Gen. 1:29) man is admonished to exercise an oversight of the earth that pleases God. This theocentric view in the P source does not allow man to exploit nature with impunity. He is called to a responsible stewardship in God's behalf.

As Elder clarified the issue on biblical grounds, Professor Thomas S. Derr of Smith College clarified it on historical and rational grounds.

> The origins of Western science and technology are multiple, complex, and obscure. It is a false simplification to identify and make prominent one particular religious strand when so many secular factors were also at work, like geography, climate, population growth, urbanism, trade, democracy, and humanistic philosophy. Besides, even if Christian doctrine had produced technological culture and its environmental troubles, one would be at a loss to understand the absence of the same result in equally Christian Eastern Europe. And conversely, if ecological disaster is a particularly Christian habit, how can one explain the disasters non-Christian cultures have visited upon

their environments? Primitive cultures, Oriental cultures, classical cultures—all show examples of human dominance over nature which has led to ecological catastrophe. (*Worldview*, Jan., 1975, p. 43.)

Historically and rationally, Derr is on target. Biblical stewardship is solidly relevant to the ecological crisis because it places human beings at the apex of creation as custodians accountable to God for their care of the earth. Equally, it avoids the dangerous unreality of making nature *without* man our moral standard. To lose sight of this biblical view of creation—as some ardent environmentalists do—is to value nature above humanity. "Triage" thinking on world hunger, for example, is unbiblical.

The valid critique of the church since the Renaissance is that it has negelcted "God in nature." It still does. Its theologians and preachers (ordained and lay) have focused attention on "God in history" (the nature and meaning of revelation), "God in personal experience" (conversion, personal ethics, existentialism) and more recently, "God in society" (social ethics, social action, political theory and practice). These emphases are biblically sound, but the church has lagged on inquiring into God in nature (exploitation of natural resources by individuals, agencies, and corporations; environmental pollution; cheapening of natural beauties; a critical examination of prayer in the light of the "new" physics; psychosomatic medicine).

Threatening current realities, more than sound biblical insights, have thrust ecology into public view. If the church had been true to a biblical stewardship, the present ecological crisis would be less acute. In that context, the church shares in contemporary society's failure to be ecologically responsible. It is unconverted man, fashioning his social structures at variance with God's order who sets loose the four horsemen of the apocalypse. Human greed for financial gain and political power, the antisocial fight for personal survival at all social levels, unbridled nationalism (national security and power), and Western man's insensitivity to the sacredness of human life have produced our late-twentieth-century tower of Babel.

Historically, it is crucial for the church to enlarge its conception and practice of stewardship to include the care of the earth in the interests of humanity. The old custom in rural parishes of blessing the fields—one way of acknowledging God's ownership of the land—might be reenacted in all congregations as a timely affirmation of our faith in a God who is active in nature for the sake of all people. It is God-in-Christ who calls us to exercise self-restraint, to improve the quality of life, and to exhibit solid respect for all life. The church, if it takes biblical stewardship seriously, will take the lead in refashioning attitudes on ecological reform. Elder argues that since a change in the human attitude "involves nothing less than a conversion . . . the church is best equipped to carry out this sort of thing." True. But first, most church members must be converted to a new concern for the God of nature.

Sound ecological teaching (responsible stewardship) must be beamed to all sectors of public life as well as to the church. The church cannot do the task alone. Massive enlightenment must be provided in and through the public schools. New skills must be developed on a broad scale in the colleges and universities if current methods of technology are to be changed and current social values are to be recast. An extensive program initiated by our representative government—local, state, federal—is also required for the effective care of the earth. Irresponsible technology, corporate capitalism, galloping nationalism, human selfishness, and the church's neglect of God in nature have converged in our time to produce the current threat to the life of one small planet, Earth. No one can turn back the clock, but we can reset it to run more closely with the time of God's creation.

It is imperative that the church challenge its members to a new life-style based on the quality of life and a respect for all life. This will be a long, hard, bitter fight in the United States, where 6 percent of the world population now uses more than 30 percent of the earth's resources. And the problem is more complex than that. Take the matter of health care, for example. In America, 60 percent of the citizens keep the other 40 percent from receiving decent health care. Professor Victor Fuchs, having examined the present health care system in the United States, declares flatly that the basic question is not what kind of health care system we should develop but what kind of society we want to build (*Who Shall Live? Health, Economics and Social Choice* [New York: Basic Books, 1975]). He argues succinctly that the hurdle in providing adequate health care is not the need for more doctors or for bigger hospitals but the need to make radical changes in our life-style (excessive eating, smoking, drinking), and to develop the willingness to come to grips with the awesome social and economic inequities in our own nation. "It is only a short walk," he observes, "from the opulence of upper Park Avenue to the rat-bitten, lead-poisoned children of East Harlem, but for our institutions that distance represents a chasm they seem powerless to bridge." Tragically, that distance exists, in varying degrees, in all American communities.

Ecological reform includes more than air and trees and mountains and rivers and oceans. It includes people, too. The church in Western society will continue to be part of the environmental problem rather than part of its solution until it persuades its own members to refashion their life-styles. It must teach its members, and they must teach others, that God expects persons everywhere to enter into his stewardship of all life or die. "Environment," Barry Commoner reminds us, "is not a motherhood issue. Pursued to its source every environmental issue generates a confrontation with . . . war, poverty, hunger, and racial antagonism." These confrontations require individuals joined into communities of faith and action which understand, appreciate, and exercise a mature stewardship of the self.

Jesus commanded his followers to love God and to love one another as each loves himself. If true community is to be established, if sermons that grapple with the issues surrounding biblical stewardship are to be preached, individual members must accept responsibility for being themselves and take up responsible places in the whole of God's creation. This is not easy for any of us. It is more to our liking to be "little gods" rather than "little Christs." This acceptance of reality is an essential strand in personal-corporate stewardship. As Paul Tillich observed, "there is nothing in man which enables God to accept him. But man must accept just this. He must accept that he is accepted; he must accept acceptance." The Christian stewardship of the self begins there. That is the thrust of the next chapter.

Chapter 3

THE STEWARDSHIP OF THE SELF

O Lord, let us not live to be useless.
—John Wesley

Christ liberates the self so each person can return to God's family and grow to authentic personhood. Through Christ, each individual enters freely into the life of God and shares in his stewardship of life. The Christian stewardship of the self—the private and public person— calls one to value, care for, and use his "given" human resources under the claims of Christ. Individuals experience healthy self-realization most fully in Christ's community, the church.

The Christian stewardship of the self, indispensable to Christian community, requires each individual to use time, human resources and experiences, and economic goods for the purposes God approves. Here, we elect to lay aside the "time, talent, and treasure" syndrome. It conditions church members against *biblical* stewardship. In church circles, the stewardship of "time" is viewed primarily in terms of service to the institutional church; the stewardship of "talent" focuses on service in the local congregation and the church-at-large; and the word "treasure" means pledging and giving to the church. Further, the process engendered by this alliterative triology opens the self to manipulation by all social institutions.

Time and the Self

No one knows when the flame of his life's brief candle, like that of the self-satisfied farmer with bulging barns, will be snuffed out. All humans are finite. Death is their common lot. God defines the issue: "you are dust, and to dust you shall return" (Gen. 3:19). Humans live in time. It is their frame of reference for understanding events, doing contemporary deeds, and planning future action. Life's cadence—birth, growth, decline, deterioration, death—spells out the flux of moments which human beings experience as the present. Time haunts human consciousness. "Time heals all wounds." "Time is money." "Time and tide wait for no man." "At that point in time . . ." "Forgive me one more time . . ." From the cradle to the grave, human beings experience time as blessing and curse.

The Bible is time-conscious. "In the beginning, God . . ." (Gen. 1:1). "For everything there is a season, and a time for every matter under heaven; a time to be born, and a time to die . . ." (Eccl. 3:1-2). "In those days a decree went out from Caesar Augustus . . ." (Luke 2:1). "Now from the sixth hour there was darkness over all the land until the ninth hour" (Matt. 27:45). "Now after the sabbath, toward the dawn of the first day of the week, Mary Magdalene and the other Mary went to see the sepulchre." (Matt. 28:1). The Bible is sensitive to time as human beings experience it, because its documents are the human record of God's dealings with persons and communities and nations in history—their time-frame.

Fate was described loosely by Werner Elert as the sum total of time which we never use fully, space which limits us to one place at any given moment, and the web of human association in which we are inextricably bound. Humans never make the best use of time. We misspend it by wallowing in the past, lamenting or rationalizing yesterday's mistakes. We distort it by glorying in an idealized past, exaggerating yesterday's successes. So we brood, so we boast. And yesterday is glued to our consciousness as tenaciously as barnacles cling to a ship's hull.

A responsible stewardship of the past is within everyone's reach because God's Spirit enables each person who is responsive to him to learn from the past without getting bogged down in it. One of Christianity's sweetest songs is "God's mercies are new to us every morning." Whoever claims the grace that liberates him from his past runs today's race without yesterday's successes and failures on his back. God blots out the failures over which we brood; he enables us to get into perspective the successes over which we boast. Freeing us from the past, he empowers us to be responsible stewards today.

Even so, the present poses hazards. William Wordsworth, distressed by the dehumanizing impact of the industrialized society in nineteenth-century England, observed: "The world is too much with us; late and soon, getting and spending, we lay waste our powers." Humans are tempted to extremes. Either we gulp the moment without savoring it and learning from it; or we squander it, behaving as though we had forever. Nonetheless, some people use the present constructively, sometimes creatively.

A creative stewardship of their present surfaced among some blacks in America in the early sixties. Their crusade was framed, of course, by history; a few slaves gaining freedom in eighteenth-century America; thousands of slaves running away in the nineteenth century; Nat Turner leading a revolt in 1831; the Civil War, 1861 to 1865; Booker T. Washington questing cautiously for human dignity in the nineteenth century; and Martin Luther King witnessing boldly at mid-twentieth century. The black freedom movement in the 1960s, while shaped by history, was nonetheless a distinctive event. It was, in the biblical sense of stewardship, a creative use of the present—God's time!

In February, 1960, four young blacks entered the F. W. Woolworth store in Greensboro, North Carolina, made several small purchases, and sat down at the lunch counter for coffee. (This brief summary is based on a report in *The Fabulous Century, 1960–1970* [New York: Time-Life Books], 1973.) They were not served. But those four blacks, freshmen at nearby North Carolina Agriculture and Technical College, remained until the store closed. The next day they returned with several companions; they were not served. They came back daily with reinforcements until half the college was asking to buy coffee at Woolworth's. They were orderly despite the taunts and insults hurled by whites who waved Confederate flags in their faces and spit on them. Their example of peaceful resistance inspired others to demonstrate. In less than a month fifteen cities in five southern states experienced black sit-ins. Then the movement surged into the North. On March 23, 1960, three hundred students from Yale University demonstrated in downtown New Haven in support of their black brothers and sisters. Several days later, four hundred civil rights protesters from Boston University, Harvard, Massachusetts Institute of Technology, and Brandeis University picketed twelve Woolworth stores in Greater Boston. Soon to explode in violence because it went unheeded, *peaceful* protest was launched because many blacks, exhibiting a new sense of the stewardship of time, had had enough of gradualism. They demanded "freedom now." They seized God's time (*kairos*).

Their protest, which mushroomed in the early 1960s, took the Establishment by surprise. John Galbraith, writing ten years after the publication of his *Affluent Society* (1959), which gave no hint of racial revolution, acknowledged that the Black Revolution of the sixties took him as well as others unawares. No one in the Establishment expected strong dissent in the 1960s. President Clark Kerr of the University of California at Berkeley predicted in early 1960 that the business community would "love the current generation of students." He announced confidently, "They're going to be easy to handle. . . . There aren't going to be any riots." But on May 13, 1960, a few months after Kerr's prediction, two hundred angry college students, protesting the House Committee on Un-American Activities investigation of communism among California professors and students, had to be dislodged from the front steps of San Francisco's city hall by police using fire hoses and night sticks. That was only the beginning. Broad social changes were effected.

The present is every person's opportunity to serve his neighbor in need. The present (*kairos*) is God's time. It is provided by him so that his people can serve him by serving other persons, which is what he wants done at all times. That understanding of the present, and use of it, is a solid strand in the Christian stewardship of time.

We must not only interpret the past and deal creatively in the present, but we must also reckon with the future. The future beguiles some into thinking that tomorrow will automatically straighten out the tangled maze of human affairs; that like the British in the nineteenth century, humanity will "muddle through." But we Americans—maimed by the immorality of the Vietnam War, disillusioned by the amorality of Watergate, and now—like other industrial nations—challenged by the new economic power (oil, copper, tungsten, and other essential elements) of Third World nations—will not be able to muddle through. The British world of 1900 is gone. Repentance and gospel faith (inseparable), a more modest national life-style, imaginative cooperation, and personal sacrifice are called for. Tomorrow will not be better unless concerned, courageous people work to make it better, employing God's time as he wants it to be used.

If the future beguiles some, it intimidates others. The Latin American theologian Rubem Alves opines that man "set in the provisional and finite context of human life, fears the future." Parents ask: What quality of life will my children experience in tomorrow's fragmented society? Older citizens ask: Will inflation pauperize me? Critical minds—looking hard-eyed at the starving Fourth World; the soaring economic strength of the Third World; the revolutionary forces in Latin America and Africa; the ineffective United Nations; and a powerful, deeply entrenched secret government at home, the CIA—inquire anxiously: Has George Orwell's 1984 come a decade early? The future intimidates many; it sobers all serious-minded people.

The biblical stewardship of time enables finite humans to face tomorrow hopefully—that is, realistically—because it assures them that Christ is in the future. When Jesus said "Do not be anxious about tomorrow. . . . Let the day's own trouble be sufficient for the day," he was not denigrating personal prudence; he was encouraging humans to break their preoccupation with tomorrow and invest their energies in living responsibly today. Obsessive concern for the past breeds nostalgia and depression; preoccupation with the future breeds neuroticism and fear. Both insulate humans against living fully in God's present.

Christ enables us to face the future expectantly: "Fear not, little flock, for it is your Father's good pleasure to give you the kingdom." Claiming that promise, the straggling bands of first- and second-century Christians were empowered to withstand the persecutions of Nero and Diocletian. Christ's promise, "Be of good cheer . . . I am with you," enabled Paul to cope with shipwreck, beatings, stonings, and betrayals without throwing in the sponge. Looking back on unrelieved hardship, Paul testified that all human hardships are slight in comparison to the weight of glory that is laid up for the faithful in God's kingdom. Christians can live fully today because they are convinced that the Christ who steadies them now will steady them in an unknown future. Death, the last dreaded enemy, need not crush the human spirit, because Christ pioneered into that unknown realm and, returning, reversed the natural process of life to death, making it now death to life for those who follow him. So, any human, born dying, passes from death into life here and now when, in his *freedom,* he gives himself to the Resurrection Christ. Christians face the future confidently because they accept the kingdom of God as a gift as well as a task. For them, it is a future hope and a present experience. Persons who follow Christ can live freely, responsibly, and expectantly because all time is in God's hands (Ps. 31:15). He wills nothing of enduring harm or injury for any in his family.

The Stewardship of Human Resources and Experience

Many parish leaders concentrate on the particular talents of various people in their congregations, coveting those talents primarily for use in and for the institutional church.

They rarely encourage talented people to serve in the community. Mary has a beautiful singing voice; she should join the choir. John is charismatic; he should work with young people. Tom has a gift with words; he should lead the evangelists. Elizabeth is a natural organizer; she should direct the every-member canvass. That is current practice throughout Protestantism. Because institutions are fashioned to get tasks done in an orderly fashion, there is the constant danger—in every area of church life—that persons will be manipulated and/or exploited in the interests of the institutional church.

Focusing exclusively on a person's talent rather than on the whole person denigrates the individual. It is necessary, of course, to take a person's talent into consideration for responsible tasks in the church—as it is in other institutions—but it is hurtful to the person and disruptive in the Christian community if the primary focus is on the talent or skill rather than on the person. Church leaders at all levels, clergy and lay alike, lag in motivating people to serve God in a broken world. They find it easier to enlist church members to serve the institutional church. This concept of stewardship is cultural, not biblical. Unless the congregation is a fellowship in which persons learn to serve God in the world, it is not practicing God's stewardship. When Jesus' disciples came to him with their discovery that other people were doing good works, Jesus advised them that God's work was being accomplished in different ways, in different places, and through persons other than themselves. Church people in every generation are inclined to limit God's liberating work to their own limited understanding of and parochial participation in it. That is natural, but it is not Christian.

Biblical stewardship also looks to God's Spirit to transform one's personal disadvantages into solid advantages for effective Christian ministry. Biblical stewardship prompts us to be especially interested in flawed persons, including ourselves. Moses stuttered. Paul had a thorn in the flesh. Luther was bad-tempered. Calvin was rigid. Contemporary church members would scarcely choose these people for places of leadership. Yet God used those flawed persons to serve humanity. Luther argued that we can afford to err in the service of God and man ("sin boldly"), because he had discovered for himself that God's overarching grace can employ human error and personal disabilities to accomplish his purposes. Christian stewardship distinguishes between the treasure and the earthen vessel. But it does not disdain *imperfect* vessels. It is God's pleasure to call flawed persons to take up his Son's ministry. After all, no one else is available! That is part of the church's stewardship.

Human resources also incorporate the whole of one's experience. The hero in *Ulysses* declares, "I am part of all that I have met." A responsible stewardship of personal success should come easily to us, but it does not. Many people fail to use their successes as learning experiences in the journey to maturity. Some people are intimidated by success, others are destroyed by it, and only a handful are matured by it. For example, strong presidential election victories maimed Grant, Hoover, Johnson, and Nixon. Minority and close elections appear to have enlarged Lincoln and Truman as persons. Christian stewardship sees *all* human "successes" as God's grace in action.

It was pointed out above that Christian stewardship enables us to learn from failure. Many moderns no longer believe that anyone learns from failure. Will America learn from its recent failures? Many think not. They point out that hope is low in all corners of our nation. Andrew Hacker, a respected American historian, argues that

America has become a nation of 200 million egos, each bent on his own purpose. Philip Slater, a distinguished sociologist, draws a grim picture of the American as defeated and disheartened, distrusting and hating his neighbor and himself—a lost being consumed by frustration and fear. Both descriptions are overdrawn, but there is jarring truth in each. (Professor Slater's *Pursuit of Loneliness* [Boston: Beacon Press, 1971] deserves a wide reading in the church. One need not agree fully with Slater to profit from his brilliant insights and judgments.)

Yet, failure, a large piece in everyone's experience, can be handled constructively in Christ's company. That is a part of biblical stewardship. Because Christianity is neither idealistic nor naturalistic in its view of human beings, it provides solid clues to what one can expect of himself and other selves in daily existence. It is the Christian God who liberates responsive people to become truly human. These liberated persons, in turn, employ their talents to fashion true community. One reason we learn slowly from failure is our pride. Ego-protectiveness blocks us from facing our part in failures. The good news motivates and enables us to accept personal and corporate responsibility for failure, offers forgiveness, provides a clean page, and equips us to begin again with new wisdom and fresh hope.

A biblical stewardship of human resources also prompts us to use our sufferings for constructive purposes. Human suffering takes many forms. It is punitive: "What a man sows, he also reaps." It is remedial: "Though he slay me, yet will I trust him." It is redemptive: "No man takes my life from me, I lay it down of my own accord." It is often inscrutable: ". . . that the works of God may be made manifest in him." Everyone, Paul declared matter-of-factly, gets his share of hardship. Suffering flattens and disables or hardens and embitters those who handle it alone. It

ennobles, enlarges, and enriches those who discern Christ
in it and give themselves to him. It was Paul's "thorn in the
flesh" that taught him to sing of God's grace. That
disability also deepened his sense of the mystery of life ("we
see through a glass dimly"). Kagawa's lectures and books
displayed a new dimension after he took up residence in
the slums of industrial Yokohama. Schweitzer's reverence
for life matured steadily after he departed Strasbourg,
Germany, to live in Lambarene, Africa. And Jesus wept
over Jerusalem and agonized at Gethsemane before he
went resolutely to the cross. Suffering, placed in God's
hands, is liberating to the self and redemptive in society.

The Christian stewardship of human resources calls us to
a responsible employment of all innate talents, developed
skills, successes, failures, hardships, and sufferings in the
service of our neighbors. This is every Christian's true
vocation. Contemporary society needs to be reminded,
especially by the church's Christ-like life-style, that the
word vocation means God's call to his people to worship
him and serve their neighbors. The Reformers understood
that. Luther announced that it is every Christian's vocation
to be a Christ-image to his neighbors. Jesus defined every
Christian's vocation comprehensively: "Love God with
your whole person and your neighbor as yourself." He also
pointed out that whatever we do for and to our neighbors,
directly and indirectly, we also do for and to him. Christian
stewardship is every Christian's primary vocation.

Possessions and Personhood

Christianity calls for the responsible management of
material goods. Biblical stewardship is concerned not only
with how we obtain material goods but equally with how we
use them. Jesus did not teach that the material is evil and

the spiritual good. He appreciated that God, having fashioned an infinite universe and having created persons in his own image, looked on his whole creation with approval, satisfaction, and joy. When man rebelled, God, in love with his chief creation, offered full pardon to man-the-rebel, coming eye to eye with him to prove he meant it! Christianity knows nothing of disembodied spirits.

Jesus' parables reflect his joyous acceptance of his Father's world. He wanted all people to have an equitable share of material goods. He also wanted them to handle their possessions in the best interests of self and other selves. Jesus did not advise Zacchaeus to get rid of the wealth which remained in his custody after his conversion. He expected him to handle it responsibly. Jesus issued no general call to asceticism. Instead, he called his disciples to obedience to God's will in their time and place according to their individual resources. So, falteringly but deliberately, Jesus' followers over the centuries have sought to serve him with their material goods.

The stewardship of money in the American church became the dominant strand in stewardship teaching after the Civil War, and especially so in the twentieth century, paralleling the growth of middle-class affluence. This is also true in our current concepts of public philanthropy and our community-wide support to meet mass human needs. These new ways for doing good to one's neighbor reflect the radical socioeconomic changes in our society. With the rise of an urban society came a money economy which emerged steadily after the fourteenth century; it dominated Western society by the late nineteenth century. During the twentieth century it spread over the world. In Western society, modern man works for money in various forms; it is the common medium of his labor. Obviously, getting and spending money is an expression and extension of one's person. When Philip Guadella had completed the research for his biography of Wellington, he stated that if he had the Duke's cancelled checks he would know what kind of man the Duke really was. The cancelled checks of church members would be revealing, too. How people in the Western world get and use money is not the only key to their character, but it is a revealing key.

Because the church, like other social institutions, needs money to function (personnel, buildings, and services for carrying on Christ's ministry in the world), stewardship teaching in the contemporary church centers almost exclusively on money, transferable property, goods, bequests, and trusts. In the social context of yesterday's rural economy and small-town culture, church members helped their hard-pressed neighbors by providing person-to-person services: food, seed, a milk cow, a barn-raising. In today's complex society, human services to needy, hurt, and wronged persons are provided through church, community, and state agencies and the courts. These services are specialized, impersonal, bureaucratically administered. The stewardship of economic goods in our society is no longer a person-to-person event.

Government's expanding role in helping the poor, the unemployed, the aging, policing giant corporations, enacting and enforcing civil rights legislation, providing educational opportunities, feeding starving peoples, narrowing the gap between rich and poor nations, etc. has increased incalculably since the Civil War. Lincoln—or Hoover for that matter—would be overwhelmed by the Washington bureaucracy of 1976. Contrary to angry charges, this expanding role of the federal government has been dictated more by phenomenal socioeconomic changes than by any particular ideology. The radical change occurred primarily in two periods of American history. The first was

1890 to 1914: the closing of the frontier, the emergence of urban-industrial society, the rise of economic imperialism, the quest for social justice, and "the war to make the world safe for democracy." The second period was 1933 to 1976: the Great Depression, public welfare, social security, World War II, the Cold War, the Fair Deal, the New Frontier, the Great Society, Watergate, the energy crisis, world hunger.

Living now in this radically changed and changing society, American Christians must work to administer public programs more responsibly and to be more innovative in providing human services to technological man. That is an essential part of Christian stewardship in 1976. The church, maturing in its concern for persons outside its own constituency, needs yet a more informed mind and a bolder way of speaking in a political society rooted in, shaped by, and dependent on an urban-technological culture. But it can only speak effectively where its life is consonant with its words.

The federal government, for example, is the only social institution that can be expected to deal directly with monopolistic corporations, giant labor organizations, and international conglomerates. But we have seen recently how well-heeled and determined lobbies for the power elite in America can influence and use the government to foster their own interests. Most political issues in our society are moral issues (budget priorities, public welfare, the size of corporate profits, the political reach of international conglomerates, the executive power of the president, nuclear armaments). The ethical decisions called for in these political areas are essential strands in Christian stewardship. The American church is up to its steeple in politics whether it wants to be or not. The only issue to be decided is whether the church will acknowledge reality and act responsibly toward persons outside its constituency.

In spite of these current realities, stewardship materials in the Protestant churches have barely begun to address them. Joseph Fletcher, presenting a paper entitled "Wealth and Taxation: the Ethics of Stewardship" a decade ago, identified this narrow institutional concept of stewardship. He revealed that when he searched the stacks of one of America's leading theological libraries where the general works on Christian social ethics and moral theology published in the last hundred years were arranged together, he found only books on church finance and money-raising for ecclesiastical enterprises. These, he said, employed the usual pitch that people should "share" their "good things" with "less fortunate" neighbors as a "duty" owed to God, who wills them to do so. Moralistic, legalistic, mechanistic, parochial, and manipulative, this ecclesiastical mind-set fosters the current unbiblical separation of stewardship from vocation in the church as well as in the world. The church does not orient to or teach biblical stewardship; it solicits money, primarily for its own institutional ends. It has produced few technical studies on fiscal policy, investment practices, business management, or general economic theory. The *enlightened mind,* no less than the *converted heart,* is essential to fashioning a sound theory and practice of Christian stewardship in the closing decades of the twentieth century. There are stirrings, but few beachheads have been secured.

Of course, the church's constituency must first be converted and enlightened. What limits the church's credibility in its peripatetic involvements in technical, economic, and political issues is its weak base of support at the grass roots and the hypocrisy of its constituency—its failure to practice within its own fellowship what it preaches. Stewardship, rooted in God's grace, issues in daily ethical acts. These Christian deeds can be examined for motives, ends, means, and social consequences. Since human motives are never pure, the maturing Christian will inquire diligently of himself whether his giving is motivated by a desire to bring God's love and justice to others. He will also examine critically the end(s) he perceives God wants to advance. These inquiries will lead him to examine not only his own priorities but also the priorities of the social institutions (church, education, government) through which he shares his money in taxes, contributions, and gifts. He will also determine whether the means he employs or endorses in institutions are consonant with the gospel. Mechanical devices, legalistic formulas, and emotional pleas which, in effect, encourage class-serving and self-justifying gifts that thwart God's grace are not supported by the New Testament documents. But the church has resorted to these unbiblical means across the centuries. The Christian steward also sees to it that his ballot supports political representatives who are concerned for justice at home and abroad.

The New Testament documents testify that Christian stewardship is motivated, guided, and undergirded by the active love of God to which persons, in their freedom, respond for the sake of persons. They demonstrate that Christian stewardship is critical-minded, bold, prodigious, and disciplined. They also demonstrate that it is social and political. Christian stewardship lives on God's grace: we love him, and others, because he first loved us. It is equally true, however, that Christian stewardship grows among people who respond to God's deed-in-Christ in disciplined ways. Cheap grace is ineffectual. Jesus put it plainly: "If you love me, you will *do* my commandments."

In the next chapter we shall attempt to put the goods-dollar aspect of this biblical view into broad historical perspective.

Chapter 4

A SUMMARY OF GIVING IN THE WESTERN CHURCH

---

*We study history not merely for amusement—
though it can be amusing—but in order to
discover how we have come to where we are.*
—*Hugh Trevor-Roper*

*The study of history is similar in approach
to that of natural science, where all discoveries
or new factual information are subject to revi-
sion, but until they are in fact revised, they
serve as accepted knowledge or truth.*
—*Carl N. Degler*

Christians in the two thousand years from the Apostolic
Age to the present have responded to God's call to
stewardship from a variety of motives and with varying
degrees of fidelity to the biblical tradition, ranging from
sacrificial commitment, the desire to earn salvation,
obedience to ecclesiastical and civil laws, and social
pressures to conscious and unconscious fear. (See Luther
P. Powell's "Stewardship in the History of the Christian
Church," in Thompson's *Stewardship in Contemporary Theology;* also, P. T. Salstrand's *History of Stewardship in the United
States* [Grand Rapids: Baker Book House, 1956]; and G. G.

Coulton's four-volume work, *Five Centuries of Religion* [New York: Cambridge University Press, 1923–1950] for detailed presentations. I am indebted to these authors, and others, for the summary in this concise presentation.)

The book of Acts and the Pauline Epistles are the primary sources for our knowledge of the philosophy and practices of material giving in the New Testament church. During the first century or two, money was given sacrificially for (a) the relief of the sick and the poor; (b) the support of the apostles, missionaries, and evangelists (Paul, Barnabas, Luke, Mark); and (c) the general expenses of public worship. In the first decades when the church was young, poor, and persecuted, giving was Christ-centered. Motivation was gratitude for God's grace. There were exceptions, of course: Annanias and Sapphira; the stingy Christians at Corinth; Demas, who "loved this present world." But those exceptions proved the early Christians' sacrificial response to God's call to do his stewardship. The early Christians, affirming that call, out-loved, out-gave, and out-died the devotees of the other world religions and local cults (T. R. Glover's classic description of the early Christians). Their stewardship, motivated by gratitude for God's-deed-in-Christ, determined their life-style. Their loyalty to Christ and their desire to share his love with others was the power in their giving not only money but self.

But as the church developed institutionally, especially after Constantine legalized Christianity, giving became less motivated by gratitude for God's grace and more by the desire to earn God's approval. By the fourth century, salvation on *merit* had become the primary motivation for giving to the ecclesiastical establishment, as it was for the Pharisee in Jesus' day. Clement of Alexandria advised Christians that "alms lighten the burden of sin." Augustine encouraged the faithful to give with "heaven's reward" in mind. Chrysostom, laying the foundation for Tetzel's extravagant claims in selling indulgences in the sixteenth century, declared that "there is no sin which alms cannot cleanse."

As early as the second century the cancerous doctrine of salvation by merit was growing in the body of the church. The malady spread unchecked through the medieval church. By the eleventh century, Pope Urban II was promising indulgences to everyone who would participate in the First Crusade against the infidels of the Ottoman empire. By the twelfth century, masses *for a price* were so deeply imbedded in the religious life of the people that the Abbot Phillippe de Harvengt protested vigorously against this unevangelical practice. Similar protests were issued during the following century. But the abuse continued. Pope Boniface VIII, in the Jubilee Year, 1300, offered indulgences to all who would make a pilgrimage to Rome with *gift in hand.* By the middle of the fifteenth century many religious institutions had so many paid-up contracts for masses that they could not meet them. In 1428 (nine decades before Luther challenged Tetzel) the papal commissioners advised the Abbot of Cluny to increase the number of monks so that the backlog of contracted agreements for saying masses for money could be honored.

In spite of rising protests, the concept and practice of salvation by merit grew steadily until, during the decadent papacy of Leo X, Luther attacked it frontally. The immediate reason for his challenge was plain. The Pope had appointed commissioners to sell indulgences throughout Catholic Europe. Albert, the new Archbishop of Mainz, had gone heavily into debt to the money-lending Fuggers of Augsburg in purchasing his appointment from Rome. (The Fuggers were the forerunners of the

Rothschilds, the Morgans, and the Rockefellers.) Pope Leo awarded Albert the profitable contract to sell indulgences in Germany, stipulating that one-half the income should go to the Fuggers for Albert's debt and the other half to Leo's personal treasury. John Tetzel, a skilled huckster of indulgences, was named collector for Saxony. Selling indulgences as "the most precious and the most noble of God's gifts," Tetzel persuaded many people that not only the sins they *had* committed but also the sins they *intended* to commit could be pardoned for a price! In addition, they could also pay off the sins of their deceased parents.

Luther, having failed to persuade area bishops that Tetzel's activities should be halted, challenged publicly this and other medieval church practices which he judged to be unbiblical. He nailed his challenge, framed as ninety-five theses for public debate, to the door of the University Church at Wittenberg. The Augustinian monk's deep Christian commitment, critical mind, resilient emotions, bold temperament, and gift for phrase-making—pitted against the seething economic, social, and political conditions in sixteenth-century Europe—fired the Reformation in Germany. What began as a dispute over a concept of stewardship ended in the formal recovery of the evangelical principle for a large segment of Christendom. (See Roland Bainton, *Here I Stand* [Apex; Nashville: Abingdon Press, 1961], chapter 10. Actually, other evidence suggests that Luther would have challenged Rome if Tetzel had never come to Saxony. But Tetzel did provide the spark for Luther's attack in 1517.)

In summary, these several observations on the concepts and practices of stewardship in the church during its first fifteen hundred years provide a solid perspective for developing a biblical view and practice of the stewardship of economic goods in the last quarter of the twentieth century. First, while the church can and does raise money by questionable methods, biblical stewardship depends on the believer's response in freedom to God's grace. Second, when the institutional church achieves strength and power, the clergy, and especially the hierarchy, tend to lose sight of the biblical truth that the church's ministry exists to serve persons. For example, both the Protestant and the Catholic churches hedged their bets carefully in the Nazi state, especially during the years 1937–1942. Both were equally protective of their institutional interests in America during the Vietnam War, especially before the Tet offensive in 1968. Third, the pressing financial requirements of the institutional church (congregational, synodical, national, global) become strong temptations to clergy and lay leaders to exploit the human motives of fear, pride, and greed, and to devise manipulative methods for getting money. Church bureaucrats and congregational leaders are regularly tempted to employ or accept practices that violate the tenets of biblical theology, fracture evangelical freedom, and demean persons.

It is in this critical context that we shall examine next the tithe as a standard of giving in the life of the church, past and present. The evidence is clear that tithing was viewed as a Christian act from the third century until the Reformation and beyond, but there is no evidence that tithing was recommended to Christians during the first several generations of the church's life. Tithing was not a widespread practice during the second century; but it became accepted in the third century. The New Testament literature neither recommends nor rejects the tithe. It appears that Jesus accepted it as a religious duty which the people "ought to have done, without neglecting the others" (Matt. 23:23).

But by the fourth century, tithing had become a common

practice, not only encouraged by the clergy but also commanded by them. Jerome, Ambrose, and Augustine approved it; indeed, they pressed for it throughout the church. In the centuries immediately after Constantine, tithing hardened into church law. By the ninth century, Charlemagne could declare that "it is ordained that every man give his tithe, and that they be distributed by the bishop's command." Because the quarrels between clergy and parishioners over tithing had become so bitter in the seventh century, the state was compelled to define the circumstances under which tithes could be ordered and collected by the church. By the eighth century, a complex legalistic and socially abrasive practice of tithing, endorsed by the state-church, had emerged.

The Reformers criticized the *required* tithe because it was not specifically called for in the New Testament. But they did not attack it frontally or persistently; they compromised. In the early days of the Reformation, Luther argued that financial support for the church should be voluntary. But the unsettled economic conditions in Germany during the first half of the sixteenth century compelled him—in his judgment—to rely on secular authorities for protection of his person and the emerging "reformation" church in Germany. At the Diet of Augsburg in 1555, the Lutheran movement was not only legalized but also granted the protection of the Lutheran princes. State support became reality; secular authority in the appointment of bishops was fixed. And a church tax for the care of local church buildings was added to the legally *required tithe*. These requirements prevailed in the lands of the Reformation on the Continent and in England, as in all the Catholic countries, into the nineteenth century.

Colonial America, which imported the state-supported church in all the royal colonies, experienced conflict over compulsory church support from the beginning. The Pilgrims (Separatists)—who had lived in the Dutch Netherlands for a generation before emigrating to New England—introduced the concept of voluntary church support on American shores. Their view did not prevail. By 1650, most churches in New England depended on public taxation. When the British took over the Dutch New Netherlands (New York), tax support for the Anglican Church was instituted immediately. Shortly after the first settlements in Virginia and the Carolinas, taxes were collected in the form of tobacco and other commodities to support the Anglican Church there. The first church-support law in Virginia was enacted by the Virginia Assembly in 1621, scarcely a decade after the first settlers had struggled heroically to hang on at Jamestown, the first permanent English settlement on the Atlantic seaboard.

There are many reasons that the stewardship of goods was at low ebb in colonial America. One was that the Old World system of compulsory church support angered and alienated the settlers. Like the majority in Europe who objected to the taxes for church support and evaded them wherever possible, the American colonials objected strenuously to coercive measures to collect money by either state or church. The classic example in colonial America is the "Parsons' Case." Shortly before the American Revolution, a drought in Virginia cut the required tithe (paid in tobacco) for the Anglican clergy in that royal colony. The clergy sued in the courts for the full amount, and the crown supported them against the people. The colonial lawyer who dared to represent the people against the king was Patrick Henry. He won. The Parsons' Case *and* Patrick Henry became prominent in America's revolutionary history.

In addition to tax support, churches in colonial society

depended on pew rents, subscription lists, lotteries, and voluntary offerings, which were meager. By their nature, pew rents (which existed in Trinity Church, Lancaster, Pennsylvania, from 1730 to 1946) throttled biblical stewardship. Pew rents also fostered class consciousness because, as in the theater, the best seats went to the biggest payers. Other stewardship practices were equally unbiblical. In 1801, concerned Lutheran clergy and laity in the eastern United States called for the establishment of a Lutheran theological seminary in America. Trinity Church declined to provide funds, stating that they had yet to pay for the tower and steeple which they had added (1785–1794) to their church, built from 1761 to 1766. To liquidate that indebtedness, the congregation's governing board persuaded the Pennsylvania State Legislature to allow them to sponsor their own lottery. Establishment of the first Lutheran school of theology in America was delayed a quarter of a century because Lutherans had little sense of biblical stewardship. In their judgment, steeples were more important than seminaries, and lotteries were more dependable than free-will giving.

During the nineteenth century the cause of world missions stirred the churches of western Europe and the United States. One segment of the American church, especially the Methodists, became aggressively home-mission–minded and followed the westward migration, 1790–1890. In varying degrees, other denominations were also stirred to serve the growing, mobile population. The calls for money beyond meeting local current needs multiplied. How would the American churches raise it? Property and money can be transferred "by theft, by chance, by exchange, and by gift," as Powell observes. The American church has regularly employed three of the four means: lotteries and other games of chance, merchandising, and free-will offerings. Washington Gladden insisted in the late nineteenth century that the church also relied on theft because it accepted money from "robber barons" like John D. Rockefeller, Sr. Some insist that all four methods are used in both Catholic and Protestant churches today. But weekly free-will giving tied to an annual pledge did not take firm root in the American Protestant church until the twentieth century, especially after World War I.

This sketch of dollar stewardship in the church over nineteen Christian centuries allows us to make several objective observations. First, motivation for giving centers in Christ, institutional needs, or ego needs. Where it does not center in Christ, abuses develop. Second, the voluntary principle in giving is strengthened in direct proportion to one's personal commitment to Christ. Third, neither manipulation nor coercion fosters Christian stewardship; instead, they obscure and smother it. Specifically, the tithe as requirement, achievement, or bargain with God is not biblical. But these misinterpretations and misuses of the tithe do not disallow the *voluntary* tithe as a legitimate strand in Christian stewardship. In the Old Testament the tithe is a testimony to God's ownership of the land; properly conceived by the Christian it is an act of worship before it is a means of support for Christ's ministry.

The voluntary tithe can be a legitimate means for fostering a Christian stewardship of money. To present this view, we need to recall the basic uses of the law in Christian context, recalling that Jesus did not destroy the law but fulfilled it. All Christians need the law for restraint, for guidance, and as a mirror which reflects their growth in Christ. At every level of Christian growth, the law, as schoolmaster, can bring them closer to Christ. Christians should not grow weary in well-doing, but they do. Christians should not ask, in the throes of hardship precipitated by following Jesus, what is going to happen to their neighbors, but they do. Paul grew weary in well-doing. Simon Peter asked, "Lord, we have forsaken all; what is our reward?" It was also Simon Peter who, advised by Christ that his (Peter's) death would be harsh, asked plaintively what would happen to John. Christians are "new creatures," but they are still creatures. They need the law for restraint and guidance.

As we observed above, there is no firm endorsement of tithing in the New Testament. It does appear, however, that Jesus, a devout Hebrew, tithed. In Old Testament times, the tithe was a foundation stone in the Hebrew theocracy. It was a legitimate tax for the support of the basic social institutions which legislated, judged, and provided social welfare in Jewish society. It also provided for the maintenance of the state-church, the religious-social institutions. As present-day Americans levy and pay taxes for the support of public institutions and public social services, the ancient Hebrews levied and paid the tithe as an appropriate means for financing their social-economic-religious institutions. But first it was a theological affirmation of God's rightful claim on land and life. Tithing was in fact part of the Hebrew's responsible citizenship as well as his religious life.

Even as this institutional responsibility was a strand in the Hebrew's good citizenship, it can be suggested that the voluntary tithe is also a legitimate evidence of responsibility in our day. Properly understood and practiced, it will not atrophy one's free response to the gospel. It can nurture it. Self-discipline is an important strand in gospel faith. Both tithing and evangelical giving can be presented in the same congregation without confusion if the presentation on tithing calls for self-discipline in freedom. Americans are not taxed by the state for the support of the church.

Voluntary tithing prods church members to consider what they ought to give as responsible persons. Pope John XXIII said, "Love is the motive and justice is the goal." That is true; yet most Christians and most citizens do not get beyond discussing both, if indeed they do that. Most citizens would not pay their taxes if the payments were not required by law and the law were not enforced by IRS agents!

The New Testament view of giving does not eliminate the *voluntary* tithe as one form of disciplined, proportionate giving, even as the gospel does not eliminate the law. Christians are saints (believers); they are not demigods. They are *new* creatures; but they are still *creatures*. Christians, restored to God's family by grace, do not become responsible family members overnight. Justification is not sanctification. The voluntary tithe (proportionate giving, discipline-in-freedom) is a legitimate Christian practice. Professor Robert Roth has identified four basic motivations in voluntary tithing: (1) thanksgiving; (2) tribute (support of priests); (3) obligation (care of the poor); and (4) obedience to God. Rightly understood and employed, the *voluntary* tithe is one means for undergirding Christ's ministry in the world and enabling the giver to grow in grace. Of course, many church members in our industrial-technological society do not have enough money to live on; others barely make ends meet. For these, the tithe would be, as it was for most church people in earlier generations, a dehumanizing burden.

Any suggestion that tithing guarantees prosperity to the practitioner is contrary not only to the gospel but also to human experience. The revived interest in tithing in the American church, especially in the decade after World War II, was fostered by a corps of earnest laypeople in the main-line Protestant churches who preached vigorously that the tithe would bring prosperity to the practitioner. Malachi 3:1, read out of biblical context, provided the sanction for this extravagant claim (recall chapter 2, section 1, on the Bible and the Word of God). Industrialist Robert Letourneau represented this attitude in the decade after World War II. He announced publicly that when he adopted the tithe his business profits surged upward and his life became well-ordered. Other prosperous laymen also offered this do-and-get witness. John D. Rockefeller, Sr., espoused the same view in the nineteenth century. He dismissed any discussion of his dog-eat-dog way of making millions by saying God gave him the money! (See Allan Nevins, *John D. Rockefeller* [New York: Harper, 1941], for a solid study of amassing and using wealth in America.) But this view is not consonant with the biblical witness. The Bible declares with jarring candor that the wicked often prosper and the righteous frequently fail. Any suggestion that tithing guarantees prosperity is unbiblical. Giving that is truly Christian is voluntary, disciplined, glad-hearted, uncalculated, and viewed as one strand in one's personal and corporate participation in Christ's ministry.

During the 1950s, a different interpretation of voluntary tithing took hold in some congregations. It focused on the word *discipline*. These congregations called for and taught disciplined giving linked with disciplined worship, Bible study, prayer, and witness. This teaching, oriented firmly to the biblical meaning of stewardship, proved to be effective in some congregations. Personally and professionally, I am committed to it. (See my *From Tradition to Mission* [Nashville: Abingdon Press, 1965], chapters 2, 3, 4.) During my three decades in the parish ministry, I have never met anyone who responded to the gospel as Zacchaeus did; neither have I known anyone who gave everything as the widow gave her mite. But I have been

85

and am privileged to work with hundreds of people who—accepting worship, Bible study, prayer, giving, evangelistic work, and person-to-person service as disciplined deeds—appreciate and demonstrate the grace of God in and through a particular congregation. They recognize that Christ's promises, separated from his demands, are "cheap grace."

Paul tells his fellow Christians to give (a) as the Lord has prospered them, (b) regularly, (c) weekly, and (d) proportionately (I Cor. 16:21; II Cor. 8:11-14). Those are firm directives; yet each person is free to respond as he will. Paul did not separate God's commands from his promises. He recognized clearly that confrontation is neither coercion nor manipulation. There is an essential difference between disciplined giving and grace giving, but the two are not antithetical. Actually, they belong together, even as law and gospel are not mutually exclusive. Christians need a measure of law (discipline) if they are to tackle God's demands seriously and accept God's grace responsibly. Warren Quanbeck, measuring stewardship against Jesus' life and teaching, observes that "the disciple is called to share the destiny of his Master which embraces suffering, rejection, death." That is every Christian's proper stewardship.

Christian stewardship begins with the existential recognition and acceptance that the servant is not above his Master. Jesus voluntarily chose the servant role. His disciples do, too. Christian stewardship requires the converted heart, the enlightened mind, the obedient will. Repentance and gospel faith; an expectant waiting on the Holy Spirit; and the humbling of self, congregation, and denomination before God are integral strands in a biblical response to God's grace. Repentance and gospel faith motivate and enable the church to participate in God's stewardship which always has a cross at the center of it.

Whoever takes up Christ's cross, denies himself daily, and follows his Lord into the world is a Christian steward. Christian life-styles differ from culture to culture, from denomination to denomination, from congregation to congregation in the same community, and from person to person in the same congregation; but obedience to Christ is the common factor in biblical stewardship. The church's responsibility, therefore, is to uncover the biblical description of stewardship, get it before its members, enable them to dig into it, and encourage them to act on it in church and society.

That is the theme of the next chapter.

Chapter 5

SOME STUBBORN QUESTIONS IN STEWARDSHIP FOR THE CHURCH

---

*Some day, after we have mastered the
winds, the waves, the tides, and gravity,
we shall harness for God the energies of
love; and then for the second time in the
history of the world man will have
discovered fire.*
—*Pierre Teilhard de Chardin*

For God so loved . . .
—*John*

American church members at present deserve the
hard-nosed criticism which Jesus leveled against his
religious contemporaries: unconcerned children at play, a
generation indifferent to socioeconomic-ecological
realities, a people unaware that the kingdom of God has
come. In pulpit and pew, in school room and public forum,
civil religion has fostered a chauvinistic nationalism; and
folk religion has formed the church's hands-off attitude
toward economics, politics, and ecology. Both have undermined the concept of the sacredness of human life.
Protestant and Catholic congregations continue to sprinkle

holy water on the *status quo*. The church in our day has not begun to "harness for God the energies of love."

In this chapter we shall identify several of the issues which point to the new climate for doing stewardship. Congregations and denominations will respond to these pressing questions in the light of the gospel as they judge best, but no congregation or denomination can evade hard questions like these and at the same time be true to the gospel and honest with history.

Are Apportionments or Quotas Valid in 1976?

Several decades ago most main-line Protestant churches raised their annual budgets under the general headings "ourselves" and "others." Lumped in the first category were staff salaries, worship and church school materials, property maintenance, utilities, etc. "Others" included the goals that had been established by the synod (diocese, district) and the national church. Little concern was shown for local needs. The "apportioned benevolence" concept worked for a decade or two until the laity and parish clergy grew restless under it. It was programmatic at best, manipulative at worst. How can one suggest that the stewardship of the mysteries of God, preaching and teaching the Word in an assembly of believers in Topeka, Kansas, is less Christian than giving dollars to share those same mysteries with people in Tokyo, Japan? All humans need the gospel. How can meeting human needs in India be more Christian than meeting human needs in the ghettos of one's own community or in Appalachia or on an Indian reservation in South Dakota? The church's mission to the world is inherent in the gospel; its concern for persons in the shadow of its steeple is also mandated by the gospel. Benevolence giving is not either-or; it is both-and.

The contemporary church must engage in a radical reexamination of how its congregations, synods, and national churches (a) build budgets, (b) solicit money, and (c) understand, teach, and practice stewardship. The mechanically devised apportionment, complete with accolades to "achieving" congregations, motivates few and alienates many in 1976.

First, an apportionment (quota) identifies Christian stewardship with secular fund-raising. It obscures biblical stewardship, which calls persons and congregations to the Christian use of God's gifts of his Word, human endowments, natural resources, and, in a money economy, cash and property.

Second, an apportionment (quota) allows the church bureaucracy to applaud those congregations which meet the apportionment in full as having fulfilled Christ's claim on them. The system—geared to 100 percent apportionment giving and thereafter to plus-giving for designated denominational objectives—encourages too many congregations to ignore the clamoring human needs in their own communities. This indifference maims the church's credibility at the grass roots. Granted, its credibility is being tested on all fronts today, but nowhere is it being tested more severely than at the level of each congregation's actual investment of human resources, physical equipment, and money to help persons *in its own fellowship* and *in its immediate community*. The awful truth is that many congregations use denominationally suggested "benevolence" to escape involvement with hard-pressed persons in their own neighborhoods.

Third, the apportionment (quota) system encourages self-righteousness in congregations and synods that meet the defined quota, which in reality is minimal for most. It engenders guilt in others. Some congregations, struggling valiantly to carry on ministries in the inner-city and in de-populated rural communities, cannot meet a mechanically devised apportionment and still serve persons in their congregations and communities. The apportionment system is inequitable; statistics based on it are misleading or meaningless.

Church bureaucracies must learn to grant freedom to each congregation (as each congregation must do with its own members) to fulfill its responsibilities locally and to share in Christ's ministry through diocesan and national channels. Christian discipline cannot be imposed. But it can be taught and learned *in freedom.* A congregation's stewardship matures in direct proportion to its relevant proclamation and teaching of the gospel in a contemporary context of clear-headed definitions of human need in the local household of faith, the local community, the nation, and the world. Christian stewardship lives in the converted heart; it is guided by the enlightened mind; it depends on the disciplined will. But it depends on God's grace. The awakening of that heart, the nurturing of that mind, and the disciplining of that will then is the purpose and result of teaching biblical stewardship.

At present all denominations are inching toward more realistic and democratic methods of budgeting. They are seeking to involve the synods (dioceses, districts) and the congregations in that process. That is simple common sense, but it is peripheral. The elemental need in the church *now* is (as it has been since colonial days) to teach biblical stewardship among the people. That task requires experienced pastors who do stewardship personally and professionally; courageous lay leaders who, as responsible stewards, are willing to confront their fellow members; theology professors who care about the parish and *participate* in its life; and church administrators who understand parish life from long and effective experience in it. The work is slow, hard, tedious. There are no shortcuts. In the long run, carping references to affluence, hysterical outcries over runaway inflation, verbal attacks on materialism, and singling out the more mature congregations for more dollars will be ineffective.

Adequate monies to do Christ's work are provided by maturing Christian stewards. The making of biblical stewards is one of the congregation's primary responsibilities. An intelligent framing and adoption of a long-range course in *teaching biblical stewardship* is every church's crucial need today. That battle will be won or lost in the local congregations. Synodical, district, diocesan, and denominational stewardship offices, increasingly concerned to be biblical, sobered by the worldwide economic climate, and appalled by social fragmentation want to help. To do that, they must encourage and enable congregations to teach biblical stewardship. (Recall chapters 1 and 2. We are not arguing in this section against the church's outreach. The parish I serve, first learning and then acting on biblical stewardship, has enlarged its annual giving from $38,000 to $435,000 over two decades. Half of that giving is outreach.)

How Shall Gifts Be Divided Between the Church and Social Agencies?

Responsible Christian citizens contribute generously to their congregations. They also contribute generously to educational institutions, social agencies which do merciful work, and political associations which promote social justice. This broad involvement is a demonstration of biblical stewardship in any society, but especially in a democratic society. How one determines the amount and distribution of his gifts reflects the maturity of his stewardship, his knowledge of human need, and his critical judgment. But some guidelines can be suggested.

First, the Christian steward does not "rob Peter to pay Paul" on any front—church, social agency, educational institution, or others. Mature Christian stewards set aside a substantial portion of their economic resources, time, and skills for creative work in all arenas where the humane interests of persons are served. Their pledge and weekly offerings to the church will be determined fairly in view of what they can give and what their congregation needs to carry on Christ's ministry in any particular year. In metropolitan areas their pledges and contributions to the United Fund will constitute a large part of their contributions outside their church giving. Even so, a solid bloc of United Fund givers also support special community services which challenge their interest (scouts, organizations for the blind, etc.); and they also support the YWCA, YMCA, Salvation Army, community centers, colleges and universities, hospitals, national centers for the prevention and cure of diseases, treatment centers, or other groups dedicated to effecting justice for people in inhumane situations.

Second, the Christian steward decides carefully where he will invest his person: as an offical board member, teacher, or choir member in his local congregation or in service on a district church board or a social agency board in his community or a public school or college board. Some church members, seeking to employ their God-given talents and developed skills responsibly, will invest more time in community service and in politics than in the *organizational* work of their local or diocesan church. That is as it should be. Every responsible congregation encourages its members to serve in the world. In fact, teaching biblical stewardship motivates people to work not only in the church but also in the world. Wherever the Christian steward serves, he will focus his energies; he will not dissipate them on too many fronts. He covets solid service rather than peripatetic activism or fleeting personal recognition.

Third, the Christian steward determines whether the church and the secular agencies he supports administer efficiently the monies they receive. Some loosely based ministries and some social agencies do not provide a sound administration of monies. Not every social agency in one's community, including some with national reputations, is competently administered. The enlightened steward sees to it that his gifts are used effectively for the purposes for which he gave them. Harvey Katz observes that charity is "big business"; on any given day of the year American contributors give "55 million dollars and countless hours of volunteer talent to charitable work." *(Give! Who Gets Your Charity Dollars?* [Anchor Books; Garden City, N.Y.: Doubleday, 1974].)

Fourth, the Christian steward does not support special interest groups in secular or ecclesiastical circles that seek to influence goals for selfish reasons. Millions of members in congregations that now have their backs to the wall must decide whether to withdraw from their congregation and unite with a servant congregation, or persevere and serve until their congregation comes alive or dies with dignity, or work for merger with another congregation(s). These decisions root in a responsible congregational stewardship of the gospel, care of persons, and in the individual's responsible stewardship of the self.

Fifth, the Christian steward does not make token gifts to the church to keep his name on its roll or to community agencies to enhance his image with his fellow citizens.

Congregations that take biblical stewardship seriously will define membership policies that call for the pastoral care of persons, foster stewardship of the self, and reflect the biblical and theological (confessional) positions to which the congregation and denomination subscribe.

Finally, the Christian steward keeps alert to leadership changes and/or faults in the leadership of his church and of the social agencies he supports. He declines to throw good money after bad even in the name of charity. In each instance of giving, recognizing that his gifts are extensions of his person, he will follow those gifts with intercessory prayer, critical inquiries, constructive suggestions, and personal participation whenever that is possible. That is a strand in responsible stewardship.

Should the Church Pay Taxes?

This question is asked more often by people in the church in the 1970s than in any previous era. Unchurched citizens have been asking it since the days of the Founding Fathers. The first step in addressing this complex issue realistically is to be factual. The institutional church pays some taxes now. Like all citizens, its members pay city, county, state, and federal taxes. Every church in the United States pays federal excise tax and federal transportation tax on all travel except that which relates specifically to education. On January 1, 1976, a corporate income tax on church-owned businesses which are not related to the church's generally accepted mission was added. Churches also pay some taxes on state and local levels. These taxes vary from one state and community to another: state and city sales taxes; taxes on certain public services; state corporate income tax on certain investments; real estate taxes on parsonages, unimproved land, parking lots, camps, and other property, depending on its use. (See Frank W. Gunn's *Churches and Taxation* [Board of Social Ministry, Lutheran Church in America, 1971], a concise, balanced study.) The real question, therefore, is: How should the churches be taxed? The total tax burden on American citizens is needlessly heavy and harshly inequitable. Tax reform and a broader tax base are needed. The pressure for both will mount steadily in this decade.

Praise the Lord for Tax Exemption, a 1969 publication, maintains that of the 32.6 percent of all United States real estate exempt from taxes, 18 percent is owned by the churches. (Martin A. Larsen and C. Stanley Lowell [Washington and New York: Robert P. Luce, 1969]. The study appears to be slanted, but it deserves to be read by clergy and lay leaders at the grass roots. A more balanced study is D. B. Robertson, *Should Churches Be Taxed?* [Philadelphia: Westminster Press, 1973].) Some dispute that claim. Nonetheless, hard-pressed American taxpayers, especially non-church citizens in our pluralistic society, are calling strongly for a broader tax base that includes churches, foundations, and other charitable and philanthropic organizations. Pressure is also increasing to lower or disallow the large deductions now granted taxpayers by the federal government for church-charity giving. State and municipal tax laws do not make these sweeping allowances. More and more citizens are convinced that the federal government should take that position, too.

Certainly one inequity, among others, in the federal income tax system is the exemption allowed on housing for the ordained clergy. It is a tax break which lay persons, even when employed by the church, do not share. It is inequitable. Honest stewardship calls the church to include this tax exemption when calculating the pastor's total annual income. It should be recognized also that the state is subsidizing the clergy as well as airlines, corporations, welfare recipients, and the Penn-Central Railroad. On the other hand, the clergy, who in fact are not self-employed, are required to pay the whole of their social security tax.

Increasingly, congregations are granting their clergy rental-utility allowances in lieu of free use of congregation-owned and maintained parsonages. Clergy use these allowances to purchase their own homes as a personal convenience, an economic hedge against inflation, and as a solid base (property taxpayer in the community) for understanding and speaking out in city, state, and nation on political issues which affect real estate values and property taxes (public housing, scattered-site housing, etc.).

On Determining the Salaries of
Full-time Church Workers

All salaries in the church should be determined openly, equitably, realistically, and honestly. Those are proper guidelines for any congregation. Openly—in consultation with the employees themselves. Equitably—fair salaries for all church employees should have a priority rating equal with benevolence payments, property maintenance, and building programs. Pauperizing any staff member (pastor, minister of education, secretary, sexton) in order to meet other pressing expenses is not honest stewardship. Realistically—according to the resources available, the total obligations of the congregation, and the professional responsibilities and competence of the salaried persons. On the other hand, if a congregation limits its benevolence giving in order to pay salaries or to meet a building debt, its leaders must ask: Should this congregation be operational?

This question will be asked increasingly by honest stewards in all congregations during this decade.

A related question on clergy salaries is being asked more frequently now. Should clergy salaries be standardized (as in the civil service and the military); and should increments be granted periodically on the basis of (a) responsibilities carried, (b) meritorious service, (c) size of congregation, (d) cost of living, (e) years of professional service? The view that salaries should be established and paid, and increased or decreased, according to church-wide standards may spread in a protracted period of unemployment and galloping inflation.

Proponents of standard salaries argue that the practice would benefit both clergy and parishioners. They judge that it would ease the tensions that exist now in many parishes between the clergy and the governing board over salary. The proponents of standard salaries point out that where staff salaries are too low some parishioners feel guilty; some offer gifts; other congregations offer larger salaries; the pastor frets or broods. They also argue that where a salary is comparatively high it causes envy (sorrow at another's good fortune) among fellow clergy and lower-income parishioners and tarnishes the service image of the clergy.

Proponents insist that standard salaries would (a) guarantee all clergy an equitable income, (b) discourage clergy from moonlighting, (c) relieve from working those parsonage wives who do not want to work for income, and (d) equalize salaries paid to female pastors.

The critics—at present the majority in main-line Protestant churches—argue that a standard clergy salary would (a) be regimentative, (b) be socialistic, (c) weaken the minister's healthy ambition, (d) reduce the congregation's incentive for growth, (e) stagnate denominations through a reduced movement of clergy among the congregations.

Lay leaders—aware that the issue of equitable remuneration for staff members has reached crisis proportions in thousands of Protestant congregations—ought to increase salaries now where incumbents merit increases. Where they do not, church-at-large officers owe it to the congregation and the pastor to help the pastor (a) improve his professional competence, (b) move, (c) find secular employment. If congregations cannot or will not pay adequate salaries, and at the same time shoulder their share of the costs of Christ's ministry beyond their parish boundaries, they may not be entitled to the service of clergy. These thrusts are strands in the church's proper stewardship.

Should Permanent Church Buildings Be Constructed?

Buildings which are crucially needed for demonstrated Christian ministries should be constructed. A sweeping moratorium on all church building is unrealistic and faithless. Some congregations need sanctuaries and /or parish houses or enlargements or renovations of present facilities now if the Christian work they are doing is to prosper. Congregations need facilities for worship, education, fellowship, and community service. These should be adequate, attractive, safe, economically operational, and designed for double and triple use on Sundays. Offices for full-time, part-time, and volunteer workers should be provided. Those who decide to build will consider operational and maintenance costs now and for the future.

A related problem in property ownership and maintenance should be indentified here: the care of historic church buildings which are increasingly costly to operate and maintain. Beginning with the handful of colonial churches on the Atlantic seaboard and following the American frontier westward until it closed in 1890, and remembering the older Spanish missions in Florida and the Southwest, one comes on historic churches that should be preserved. They are a precious part of our American heritage. Those that are designated as historic buildings will require, in some cases, large expenditures of money for maintenance and preservation. The economic responsibility should rest with (a) the congregation, (b) the denomination, (c) the community, and (d) the state. The Bicentennial Year is an auspicious time to alert congregations, denominations, communities, and the state that they have a joint obligation to forebears and descendants to exercise a proper stewardship over *historic* churches.

Should Everyone Pledge?

Church members *should* pledge a part of their resources annually so that the church can operate without bickering over money. In all Christian churches a salaried leadership, buildings, equipment, and programs cost money. The church's leadership should not be compelled situationally to spend hours haggling over dollars; every member should feel he or she has a stake in providing Christ's ministry in and through a particular congregation.

Second, church members *should* pledge from their resources because the self-discipline is a constructive strand in fashioning wholesome personhood. Americans are quick to point out that discipline without freedom ends in personal and social tyranny. It is equally true, however, that freedom without discipline ends in personal and social anarchy. That is one reason that Jesus, accepting human freedom, called vigorously for self-discipline.

Third, money, checks, notes, mortgages, installment buying, sales contracts, credit cards, and automatic bank payments are the personal promises on which our social structure is based. The institutional church deserves at least the same support that department stores, banks, auto agencies, and service stations receive from church members! In a promissory (pledge) economic culture, it is prejudicial for any church member to exclude the church. The casual response of some church members, "I never pledge, but I give what I can," means in effect that they have "pledged" so much money for houses and food and clothing and cars and boats and alcohol that few of their dollars ever find their way into churches and charities.

Finally, since a church pledge is not a legal obligation, the objection "I don't pledge because I may not be able to keep my pledge" is evasive. If the objector has never taken out a mortgage or negotiated a bank loan or opened a charge account in a department store or asked for credit from anyone, but instead pays cash for everything, he has a situational case against pledging! In 1976, few Americans can make that claim. The constituencies of main-line Protestantism do not go cash all the way. When, because of extended illness, unemployment, or any hardship, a church member cannot maintain his pledge, he simply advises his church of his altered economic situation. No congregation presses its members for unpaid pledges; each hard-pressed member is met compassionately.

Some congregations place this sentence on their printed pledge cards: "It is understood that I (we) may decrease (increase) this pledge as reduced (increased) economic circumstances dictate." Church members *should* pledge and give as God has prospered them.

Should Everyone Tithe?

We observed in the last chapter that many people cannot tithe because they do not have enough money for proper housing, food, clothing, medical care, and education for their children. Nonetheless, the contributions some poor people make to the church and to charitable agencies, while limited in amount, are sacrificial. These people should be encouraged to pledge what they can, and their gifts should be acknowledged gratefully. Some economically poor people make more generous gifts to the Christian church than many of its affluent middle-class members.

Perhaps a third—some say a half—of main-line Protestant church members could tithe without altering substantially their present comfortable or affluent life-styles. But to expect that many comfort-saturated, pleasure-oriented church members will jump from minimal giving to the tithe and beyond without intermediate steps is unrealistic. To encourage people to give a definite percentage of their gross or net income and to persuade them to reconsider their level of giving annually in the light of God's goodness is a tactic in Christian discipline. Those members who do give 5 percent or 10 percent or more of their gross or net incomes do not entrust the total amount to the church but also share part of it with secular social agencies, colleges, political parties, and private deeds of compassion. That is *biblical* stewardship.

Finally, the tithe is not an adequate measure of giving for several millions of church members. Some who began by giving 5 percent and moved to 10 percent have gone on to 15 percent and more. One family I know gives 30 percent of its net income. They began years ago by tithing. People grow through Christian discipline in grace. The tithe should not be employed as an end in itself. But viewed as a voluntary exercise in disciplined giving, it will be for many "the first reasonable step in Christian giving."

Should Pledges and Annual Gifts
Be Published with Names?

Each individual is free to reveal what he gives, but a congregational publication which lists the names of contributors and the amounts they give violates human freedom. The Internal Revenue Service promises to respect the taxpayer's privacy; it has failed to do so. The church should be more dependable. The elected lay officers and the clergy require access to recorded pledges and contributions for pastoral and administrative purposes; others do not. The old saw, "If you're not afraid to let God know your giving level, you shouldn't be afraid to let others know it, too" is fatuous. A published list of givers and gift amounts is coercive.

What Belongs to God?
What Belongs to Caesar (State)?

This may be the most stubborn and disruptive stewardship question Christians face in this decade. Responsible Christians are responsible citizens. They make sustained efforts to understand and decide socioeconomic-political issues in the light of God's Word.

This brief historical background will provide broad guidelines for getting at this significant strand in biblical stewardship. (See my *Politics, Poker, and Piety* [Nashville: Abingdon Press, 1972], for a full treatment of this crucial theme.)

From Nero to Diocletian, Christians in the Roman Empire were subject to sporadic persecutions. These government-sponsored attacks ended in the fourth century A.D. when the Emperor Constantine legalized Christianity. Church membership soared. By the high Middle Ages, the whole of western Europe was nominally Christian. The

Bishops of Rome had claimed for centuries that Constantine had transferred not only the spiritual but also the secular rule of the West to them, though "the Donation of Constantine" was exposed as a forgery in the fifteenth century. The emergence of modern nation-states and the Reformation ended the notion of *one* church and *one* empire in fact. After the Reformation, each national state established a particular church by law. State control over the organization of the churches expanded. By the seventeenth and eighteenth centuries both Catholic and Protestant political rulers, arguing the divine right of kings, had made the church subservient to the state. As the state's power grew, the churches relaxed their beliefs; dissenters were tolerated because the state insisted on it. This European experience was transplanted to North American shores during the period of colonization, 1500–1775, by the Spanish, French, Dutch, English, and Germans.

The colonists, emigrating from different European nations, brought a diversity of Christian traditions to America. Some colonies (Massachusetts, New York, Virginia) had established churches—state churches. Others (Rhode Island, Pennsylvania, Maryland) developed a measure of religious freedom. When the federal Constitution and the first ten amendments became operative in the 1790s, it was no longer possible to establish a state church in the United States. Consequently, Article VI of the Constitution reads: "No religious test shall ever be required as a qualification to any office of public trust under the United States." The First Amendment declares that Congress shall not interfere with freedom of religion, speech, or press, assembly, and petition.

Under the Constitution the several states were free to work out these matters for themselves. State support for any church (Massachusetts) ended in the United States in 1833. Religious tests for office holders remained, however, in state constitutions for decades, and hundreds of blue laws were enacted by the several states during the nineteenth century. State laws calling for prayer and Bible-reading in the public schools were common until the mid-twentieth century. These laws were not challenged strongly as long as the United States was "Protestant" in sentiment. But that sentiment was inundated by the heavy immigration from Ireland and southern Europe after the Civil War. The new minorities—appealing to the Fourteenth Amendment to the Constitution (ratified in 1868 to safeguard the civil rights of blacks) and to the First Amendment—insisted on their rights in an increasingly pluralistic society.

Religious pluralism in America has multiple roots: (a) the diversity of denominations and sects (235-plus); (b) the disestablishment of state churches; (c) the periodic evangelistic revivals (1740 to the present) which stressed personal commitment to Christ; (d) the leveling forces of the frontier until 1890; (e) the democratizing impact of Jacksonian ideology; (f) the extension of the voting franchise; (g) the economic opportunities provided by an expanding industrial society which opened an upward socioeconomic mobility. Until the end of the nineteenth century Protestantism was the dominant religion in America, and as such, affected strongly the nation's aspirations, values, life-style, and enacted laws. But by 1950 religious pluralism in America was recognized if not everywhere accepted. The issue of church and state, Christ and culture, an old chestnut in medieval and modern European history, is a live issue in America. H. Richard Niebuhr identifies this centuries-old issue as "the double wrestle of the church with its Lord and with the cultural society with which it lives." Oscar Cullman concludes that "the question of church and state is so closely bound up with the gospel itself that they emerge together."

Thus in the cross of Christ the relationship between "Christ and Caesar" stands at once in the beginning and at the center of the Christian faith. As a corollary, the problem, "Church and State," is posed for the Church at all times, forever: "For my sake you will be dragged before princes and kings, to bear witness before them and the gentiles" (Matt. 10:18). This does not mean that the Church must of necessity be persecuted by the State: it does mean, however, that it must always reckon with the fact that it *can* be persecuted by the State. The cross of Christ should lead the Church in all its deliberations about the relationship of Church and State; not just in its negative aspects, but in its positive aspects as well. (Oscar Cullman, *The State in the New Testament* [New York: Scribner's, 1956])

American Christians are now faced with the complex task of (1) getting free from simplistic views of the relationship between Christ and culture and facing the ambiguous interactions between church and state; (2) accepting that politics is one viable means for creating a more humane society; (3) bringing factual knowledge, courage, and integrity to bear on political decision-making in a society which currently is both free and totalitarian; and (4) discerning God at work in the ambiguities of history.

American Christians now engaged in church-state discussions must also learn that Christianity is supra-national. The issue is not only "church and state," it is "church and *states*." Alan Geyer reminds us that most church-state doctrines "are purely domesticated in trying to locate Christianity somewhere within the state . . . . The church has a trans-national life which touches a vast plurality of states."

Paul, rejecting monasticism, sectarianism, and syncretism, laid the foundation for the doctrine of "the two kingdoms": church and state(s)—in tension. The Christian has obligations to both, but his first allegiance in any conflict which he perceives between the two belongs to neither *per se;* it belongs to God. His active witness may or may not alter the secular (state) mind, but each Christian is obligated nonetheless to make that witness. A solid chance to transform society rests with Christians who not only employ political means to create a humane society, but also with those who dissent from and resist policies and deeds of the state which dehumanize society.

Thomas Jefferson, fearing the reenactment of the religious persecutions of Europe on American shores, authored the Statute of Religious Freedom in Virginia (1786). He insisted vigorously on an amendment to the federal Constitution which provided for this separation of church and state. Like Paul, Jefferson accepted and supported the view that churchmen (citizens) will address those political and social issues which concern them.

Interaction between the institutions of church and state is inevitable; church members are citizens of the state. The institutions of church and state interact on each other through their human constituencies. The dean of American church historians, Sydney Mead, reminds us that churchmen joined actively with non-churchmen in building the American political society on the foundations of England's Atlantic community. Only in the twentieth century did the church in America retreat from recognizing this involvement. The church's flight from political responsiblity in the twentieth century is not biblical; it is not constitutional; it is not realistic. Practical politics and Christian convictions cannot be compartmentalized. Our forebears recognized, accepted, and acted on that reality. Church members are now being forced to reexamine the proper relationship between church and state on biblical, theological, constitutional, sociological, and psychological grounds.

In early Hebrew history, loyalty to God and to his chosen people—the nation—were indentical. First and Second Kings and Chronicles present the view that the Lord of hosts helps the Israelites triumph over their enemies. Yet even in those crude nationalistic-religious stories there are hints that God helps only those nations which are loyal to him. Joshua, for example, opposed a nationalistic war because God disapproved it. The eighth-century prophets refined and enlarged that view. They saw God standing over and above their own nation, judging it severely for its disregard of his purposes. Jeremiah's reference to God's plumb line reflects this view. Jesus accepted and then expanded this prophetic view to universal proportions: God invites and requires a loyalty which transcends not only one's loyalty to nation but also to race, color, sex, generation, tranditional beliefs, and family. He defined God's community as supra-national, supra-racial, supra-regional, supra-class, supra-family, supra-church.

This bold teaching, challenging the narrow religious outlook of the Pharisees, set them against Jesus. Inevitably, his teaching collided with the sovereign claims of Rome. The Pharisees, determined to destroy Jesus, asked whether a Jewish citizen should give primary allegiance to Caesar (Rome ruled Judea) or to God. Jesus responded by asking for a coin of the realm and inquiring whose inscription was on it. His adversaries answered, "Caesar's." Jesus' counsel went to the heart of the issue: "Render to Caesar the things that are Caesar's and to God the things that are God's." Each person must judge for himself which loyalty he will opt for in constantly changing historical situations. God is not totalitarian; he allows each person to decide his own allegiances. But Jesus made it plain that one has solid obligations to the state as well as to God. Each must discern those obligations for himself and act on them. The church member who seeks to avoid political responsibilities is neither a good Christian nor a good citizen.

But how does one discern in any particular moment of history what belongs to the state and what belongs to God? Simon Peter, proclaiming Christ in an alien Roman culture and a hostile Jewish society, argued that Christians are called to obey God rather than men. That means clearly that the Christian dissents from and resists every directive from any individual or association of persons (ecclesiastical or political) which requires him to speak or act contrary to his conscience under God. For Simon Peter, and for thousands more in the first several centuries of Christian history, the price of a conscience bound to Christ was death. That was the price Dietrich Bonhoeffer and Martin Luther King also paid. Yet between Paul and Peter, Bonhoeffer and King, men like Tertullian and Augustine, Aquinas and Luther, Calvin and Cromwell managed to live creatively with severe conflicts between church and state.

There are no fixed answers to the crucial issue before us, however much we yearn for them. Socrates, Plato, Aristotle, Locke, and Jefferson failed to reconcile personal liberty with the state's authority. Hobbes and Lenin, ignoring personal liberty, argued the state's case. They also failed. "To face the problem of Man vs. the State is to recognize the uniform failure of political philosophy to solve it—or even to confront it" (Milton Mayer, *On Liberty: Man v. The State* [Santa Barbara: The Center for the Study of Democratic Institutions, 1969]).

Jesus provides the one realistic approach: since every citizen's personal liberty and the state's authority exist in tension, each Christian must decide his allegiances and establish priorities in the context of his loyalty to God, his concern for humanity, and the ambiguities of history. More than that is tyranny of the human spirit. Less than that is irresponsibility to God, self, and society.

Other questions related to the issues of church and state which we have not outlined above come readily to mind. Abortion, euthanasia, eugenic engineering, public welfare, military spending, internal security (invasions of privacy), control of the news, civil religion, religious use of the communications media, prison reform, international conglomerates, public and private education, care of the aging, poverty (the distribution of wealth), the rights of minorities, consumer rights, world hunger, population control, the emerging Fourth World, nuclear arms control, censorship, and firearms control are moral-social-political issues which the church must address and act on in concert with others wherever it does God's stewardship.

New Opportunities

God's grace covers us; his power in Christ is available. That is the church's solid ground for hope in this or any era of history. Will the church take seriously the stewardship of the mysteries of God, human resources, and human gifts? Will it teach *that* stewardship in word and deed first in its congregations and through them in the world? Having missed scores of opportunities to serve God in the tumultuous decades of changes in this twentieth century, the church can yet go before the tribunal of biblical evidence and rediscover there that its mission is to do God's stewardship in the world.

Millions of church members, gathered in thousands of congregations, are free to determine whether they will take up Christ's ministry in the world or live for themselves behind stained glass windows that shut the world out. That makes human freedom "dreadful freedom" indeed.

Appendix 1

ONE WAY TO USE THIS STUDY

These suggestions for using this book may be helpful.

First, pray daily and specifically for the gifts of the Spirit. In all corners of the church today, we plan more than we pray. We cast the burdens of the world on our own shoulders and, however resolutely we press on, finally go down under the weight of them. We have not in the church, because we ask not.

Second, see that the action begins with the elected lay leaders of the congregation—clergy, church council, church school superintendent, and officers of the several auxiliaries. Most church councils and other elected lay leaders in the congregations can, when they put their mind to it, complete their business meetings in an hour or so and thereafter give another hour and a half to the study and discussion of biblical theology and its implications for their congregation's ministries in the world. This period will allow for five or six sessions for a study like this and, in other years, for studies on evangelism, church and state, specific social issues, the doctrine of the Word of God, selected books of the Bible. The leader for the study sessions in the council may be the pastor or a lay person or a mutually agreed on lay person or pastor from the church-at-large or another congregation. Different lay persons may also present the several chapters. Some church councils will be tempted to skim chapters 1 and 2. If they succumb to that temptation, their inquiry into biblical stewardship will be distorted. There are no shortcuts.

Third, confrontations between persons and groups grow out of serious conversations that are oriented to God's Word. Let them occur. Paul tells how he withstood Peter to his face over the universality of the gospel (Gal. 2:11). Hard questions must be faced first in the council sessions and thereafter in the congregation itself. Are the clerical and lay leaders in our congregation maturing stewards of the gospel? Are they wedded to the social *status quo*? Concretely, what does our congregation risk for Christ? What will it risk? The blind cannot lead the blind. Is our congregation actively concerned about hard-pressed people in our community and throughout the world? The insensitive and unimaginative cannot help wounded persons. Does our congregation, through its preaching, teaching, pastoral care, and outreach (personal evangelism and social action) coddle and weaken or comfort and strengthen its members? The bland cannot lead the bland. Other hard questions, several of which are identified specifically in chapter 5, must also be faced. Jesus' judgment that anyone who sets out deliberately to save his life will lose it is as applicable to congregations as to persons. Conflict is inevitable among human beings who seek to take seriously the whole counsel of God. But under God, conflict can be healing, creative, redemptive. Where church leaders and members cannot handle conflict creatively, they deny the power of God's Word in their own lives. (See my *Preface to Parish Renewal* [Nashville: Abingdon Press, 1968], especially chapters 4 and 5.)

Fourth, be honest, forthright, patient, and kind with one another. Jesus said, "Woe unto you . . . hypocrites." He also prayed, "Father, forgive them; they know not what they do." The church always finds it easier to talk about Jesus than to follow him.

Fifth, when the elected lay leaders of the congregation

have completed their study sessions, the congregation should be given planned opportunities to discern and wrestle with the concept of biblical stewardship and to probe its implications for their life together in the world. The best way to introduce this study in many congregations is through a series of teaching sermons. Three decades ago, C. H. Dodd pointed up the contrast between essential gospel facts (the content of preaching in the Early Church) and theological and ethical applications of those gospel facts (the content of teaching in the Early Church.) That is a proper academic distinction. But in the life of the church, biblical preaching, like evangelical teaching, incorporates both promise and demand. Promise without demand becomes cheap grace; demand without promise becomes legalism. Promise and demand form the content in both the preaching and teaching functions of Jesus' ministry. It is also recorded (Acts) that the Apostles "did not cease to preach and teach Christ daily." The pulpit is the focal point—but not the only place—for proclaiming *and* teaching both the promises and demands of God in the congregation. In most congregations it is the best place for introducing this study to the whole congregation.

Some pastors may find this series of *teaching* sermons to their liking: "The Changing Climate for Stewardship in the Church"; "Toward a Christian Life-Style"; "God's Steward: Converted Heart, Enlightened Mind, and Disciplined Will"; and "Jesus' Love of Life." Other themes surface in the five chapters: "The Old Testament Concept of Stewardship," "Jesus' Teaching on Stewardship," "Paul's Teaching on Stewardship," "Is the Tithe Legalistic?" "The Church's Proper Custodianship of the Gospel," "The Meaning of Revelation," "Schweitzer Remembered: Respect for Life," "God's Time: Our Stewardship of the Present," "A Christian Stewardship of Suffering," "A

Christian Stewardship of Failure," "If Our Canceled Checks Could Talk," "The National Budget and Biblical Stewardship," "Planned Giving of Time and Money," "Can One be Christian and Patriotic at the Same Time?" "On Going the First Mile," "How Far Is the Second Mile?" Pastors, in dialogue with their lay leaders, will introduce the study to suit their particular situations.

Thereafter, the content of chapters 1 to 5 can be taught in adult classes or the adult forum of the Sunday church school or in small groups during the week. Lay persons who are mature stewards, prepared to present the material, can serve as the teachers. There are special gains, however, if council persons do the teaching. A mimeographed summary of the material to be presented (prepared by the pastor and a council-congregational committee) should be provided at each session. Five or six teaching sessions are suggested, chapters 1 to 5 providing the substance for the lecture-discussion or panel-question format. In congregations of one or two hundred confirmed members, the pastor, church council, and a half dozen parishioners may study the material and then conduct small group meetings in the homes of the parish.

Finally, every congregation should have a stewardship committee. It should (a) be peopled with mature stewards, (b) provide regular opportunities for the congregation to learn biblical stewardship, and (c) handle the mechanics of pledging and giving. But Christian stewardship is the ongoing responsibility of the whole congregation. It cannot be delegated to a committee. Tragically, the stewardship committee—like the evangelism committee—in many congregations comprises people who are interested in "that sort of thing." That attitude must be challenged; biblical stewardship and evangelism must be taught boldly if those congregations are to exercise God's stewardship.

Appendix 2

SOME TESTED WAYS OF DOING "DOLLAR" STEWARDSHIP

The more successfully the good
and right assume concrete form,
the more they become evil and wrong.
—*Karl Marx*

In the beginning was the Word. . . .
And the Word became flesh.
—*John*

In this Appendix we have cataloged and commented on some ways of doing "dollar" stewardship (raising the congregational budget). Congregations, like people, differ in faith, resources, temperament, outlook, and situation; what works in one may not work in another. Consequently, the leadership in each congregation should examine, adapt, and employ those methods which provide suitable vehicles for chaneling the dynamics of biblical stewardship in and through their congregation. But methods, however sound, do not motivate people to give. That is the work of the Spirit through the Word in proclamation, teaching, dialogue, and deed.

The Every-Member Response

This method has been used in some congregations for a half century. (The First Evangelical Lutheran Church, Greensburg, Pennsylvania, has used the EMV since the mid 1920s. My father, canvass chairman for years, drew me into it as a lay visitor when I was sixteen years of age!) In 1976, it is the most widely used method in main-line Protestantism. Nonetheless, if the every-member approach is to be effective, lay visitors must be mature stewards, effective communicators, and persuasive witnesses to Christ. It is not enough that the visitors are pleasant people willing to make three or four casual visits to fellow members, which is a reasonable description of the EMV in most parishes.

Too often the conversation between visitor and visited deteriorates into a gripe session about the church, pastor, council, or an auxiliary. Frequently, this is a calculated deed to escape pledging. If the complaint is legitimate, the visitor will discuss it briefly, encourage his fellow member to discuss it with the pastor or a council member, then get to the matter at hand: the presentation of the congregation's ministry and the receipt of a responsible pledge. If the complaint is unfair, the visitor will say so graciously but firmly. Healthy congregations provide regular opportunities for members to get things off their chest: monthly sessions of "coffee and conversation with the clergy," personal conversations with the clergy, and regular opportunities for organizations and individuals to attend church council meetings. Every parishioner should be encouraged to have his or her council person to whom concerns are expressed. Communication should be quick, direct, and responsible. But the every-member canvass is designed for dialogue on dollar stewardship in biblical context.

Unless the congregation is visited regularly at other times of the year by the clergy and laity, it will be difficult for the visitors to focus on the primary tasks: to encourage a responsible stewardship of dollars and to receive realistic pledges for the coming year. Set in the larger context of biblical stewardship taught throughout the year, those are the proper goals. The general criticism of the every-member canvass is that it is casual rather than purposeful, formal rather than existential, cultural rather than biblical. The corrective is obvious: teach the visitors biblical stewardship and equip them to teach it in the parish. That is a never-ending task.

Pledging at Worship Services

This means for underwriting the annual congregational budget has become widely employed in main-line Protestant churches during the last decade. Augmented by mail-pledging, it is likely to be used more extensively in the years ahead because (a) pledging as an act of worship is more meaningful to most people in the hour of corporate worship, (b) confidentiality in pledging is guaranteed, (c) little organization is required, (d) the stewardship sermon allows God's Word to bear on human lives in the hour of pledging.

But this method has limitations, too. Unless the congregation worships regularly; unless biblical stewardship is preached, taught, and acted out year round; unless the stewardship sermon is a proclamation of the gospel rather than a sales pitch to underwrite the budget; unless the stewardship of money is related integrally to the congregation's stewardship of God's Word; and unless the budget has been constructed responsibly and presented concretely to the critical satisfaction of the church members, pledging at church services will be little more than parish housekeeping.

On the other hand, this means for underwriting the congregational budget is solidly effective in parish situations where budgeting is done realistically; the full membership has an opportunity to study and question any item in the budget; and the congregation is maturing in disciplined worship, giving, and witnessing.

Pledging at a Congregational Dinner

This method for underwritng the congregation's annual budget is effective in some parishes. It may be especially useful during the first several years of a new pastorate. It is readily usable in smaller congregations. But some large congregations also employ it by scheduling a series of congregational dinners, attendance at each being defined by alphabet or geography. A few suggest that the attendances should be defined by the participants' general levels of giving. Most, however, judge that each of the dinners (in a large congregation) should be representative of the whole congregation. To assemble big givers, modest givers, and small givers in homogeneous conclaves apes some secular campaigns. The procedure is scarcely Christian.

It is difficult to finance any voluntary institution these days—especially the church—in a truly Christian fashion. All congregations fail at it somewhere; too many congregations fail at it everywhere. What is tragic, however, is that some congregations do not care how they get dollars so long as they get enough to maintain their parochial existence and support their family chaplain.

Pledging by Mail

Some Protestant congregations employ this means of underwriting the annual congregational budget. Professionally, I had firsthand experience with it in Christ (College) Church, Gettysburg, Pennsylvania, two decades ago. It worked because the congregation was homogeneous (seminary and college professors, seminary and college students, and middle-class town people), and the congregation had a year-round program for teaching stewardship. Generally, however, pledging at worship services or use of the every-member canvass appears to be more effective means.

Nonetheless, it is likely that in the next few years more congregations, depending on where their members live, will adopt some method of pledging by mail because of transportation costs and their members' erratic participation in weekly worship services. This could compound their problems as *congregations*.

Pledging One's Time and Talent

Some congregations provide opportunities for their members to pledge some specific personal service to the congregation as well as their money. This procedure is effective if the teaching of biblical stewardship is a vigorous strand in the congregation's life. Otherwise, the practice is one more manipulative device which matches people to "church jobs." Common sense suggests that linking this particular pledge with the pledge of money may be deflective. The focus in subscribing the annual congregational budget should be, without apology, *on money*. (Recall chapters 1–5 for the context in which this blunt observation is made.) Giving solidly is a reflection of human time and talent, an extension of one's person.

Employing Fund Directors

Many congregations testify that they have benefited from working with sensitive fund-raisers. Even so, a congregation is well advised to proceed with caution in getting a fund director. The parish leaders will ask pointedly and discuss openly these and related questions: (1) Can our members do the task themselves? (2) Would our leaders mature if they did it themselves? (3) Does our congregation want and will it accept outside help? (4) Does our pastor really want outside help? (5) Is the proposed fund-raiser compatible with our congregation's leadership? (6) Is the fund-raiser's firm reputable and responsive to the stewardship teaching thrusts in our congregation? (7) Will our elected lay leaders prepare the congregation for the specialist and then follow up the appeal soundly? (8) Are our clerical and lay leaders evading their responsibilities? Number 8 is crucial; it should be probed relentlessly, discussed fully, and decided honestly. Congregations, satisfied that they fulfill these requirements, will benefit in varying degrees from working with competent, committed, compatible fund-raisers.

Nonetheless, many congregations would mature more steadily if they engaged the services of a dedicated, competent, analytical, articulate parish generalist as a parish *consultant* for a week or two of concentrated study, teaching, preaching, conversation, evaluation, and shared decision-making in *all* areas of congregational life.

Mass-Printed Materials

Such materials are useful in many congregations. Content, format, and style determine which mass-produced stewardship materials are used and how they are used in any congregation. The cultural disposition of each congregation is a deciding factor in choosing printed stewardship aids. Materials that are helpful in a three-hundred-member Southern Baptist church in Oxford, Mississippi, may not be equally useful in a two-thousand-member Episcopal church in San Francisco.

The bulk of the printed stewardship materials used in main-line Protestant churches a decade or two ago was shallow in biblical content, narrowly institutional, and promotional. In 1976, the major denominations are producing some materials that are biblically solid, theologically sophisticated, culturally sensitive, psychologically sound, and low-key. Critically selected, these materials are useful in most congregations. But every congregation should try its hand at producing its own material, too.

One congregation I know produces its own stewardship material: a four-page printed folder with (1) a brief message from the lay chairperson on page 1; (2) the current and benevolence budgets on pages 2 and 3; and (3) a listing of staff and vestry pledges (without names) for the coming year on page 4. The material is simple, economical, and integral to this congregation's life-style. The congregation also uses general church literature in other seasons of the year.

Bingo, Bazaars, and Banquets

Bingo, played in many parish houses across America, provides millions of dollars for several segments of the Christian church. It is true that these games of chance, responsibly supervised, provide entertainment and a limited social involvement for many middle-aged and older people. In some communities, young couples play bingo to furnish their kitchens! The money collected from these games is used for worthy purposes in and through the church. Nonetheless, several stubborn questions surface. Is this particular means as Christian as the ends for which the money is used? Does it blunt the teaching of biblical stewardship? Lotteries and other games of chance have been used in the past, especially in colonial America. Many Christians, however, are not able to reconcile any game of chance with biblical stewardship.

Bazaars are popular in some congregations throughout the United States. The monies raised through these organized activities are put to good use in and through the church. Bazaars also provide opportunities for fellowship. Properly conceived and directed, a bazaar can be a *preliminary* stewardship event in economically hard-pressed parishes where the church members have not yet become involved in service to others. A Lutheran pastor in upper New York state, writing about his two-pronged task in motivating a spiritually apathetic and economically depressed congregation to take up Christ's ministry more vigorously, described his employment of the bazaar.

> My second task, as I saw it, was to make the people start doing. They didn't have much to give financially, but they had two things going for them. They had the ability to work and they had a building. I proposed to them that they begin using these two things in the service of the Lord. It was thus that we started working on a charity bazaar. It was to be a crafts bazaar. Literally everyone in the congregation came on board for this event. I had women sewing, knitting, painting, anything that they were good at. If they didn't know how to do anything, I brought people in to teach them how. I put the men to work making toys and collecting finished articles. We worked like this for six months. On the day of the bazaar, we raised $1,710.00 and sent every dime of it for American Missions. For the first time in nearly half a century, the people of Zion had done something together for others. They are still high from the experience.

Bazaars, street fairs, house-and-garden tours, and similar events do provide the means for raising money for benevolence and charitable objectives. They also foster neighborliness. In some situations, they can be the beginning of new life for depressed congregations. However, they should serve to prod lagging congregations to get at biblical stewardship or be used supplementally in congregations already maturing in biblical stewardship.

Banquets—church dinners, hot lunches, salad bars, and strawberry festivals open to the community—remain a means of raising money in many congregations throughout the nation. Church suppers are not as popular as they were during the Great Depression or during the "fellowshipping" 1950s, but a number of churches still employ them for raising money. The money is put to good use in and through the church. A degree of fellowship marks the event. Members invest their time and skills in preparing the food and confections. Again, however, one will inquire whether the time expended in these activities could have been employed more profitably for Christ in person-to-person evangelism, Bible study groups, or some other basic function of Christ's ministry. One will also ask whether these activities dull the edge of teaching biblical stewardship. If the worldwide economic situation worsens, it is likely that these means will be renewed in many congregations.

None of these means has been used at Trinity Church during the last half century, although fellowship suppers are occasional strands in the regular teaching sessions of the church's ministry. My two immediate predecessors (1920–52) instituted first the weekly envelope and then the pledge card. My professional judgment is that pledge cards and envelopes are solid aids in teaching and doing dollar stewardship.

Parish situations and community mores vary throughout America. There is no standard way to do dollar stewardship. Gifts that are proportionate, regular, motivated by one's love for Christ and rooted in one's desire to help hard-pressed neighbors are pleasing to God. Those are proper criteria for assessing the way any congregation does stewardship.

The Covenant Church

The Judeo-Christian faith witnesses to the God who makes covenants with willing believers. It is only because God first acted in our behalf, offered amnesty to us rebels, agreed to covenant with us, that any one of us can commit himself to Christ. The decision, made in freedom, to discipline one's self according to the divine promises and demands is at the heart of Christian faith and life. A strand in this covenanting process is the pledging and giving of money for Christ's ministry in and through his church.

During the last decade a few congregations—stirred by awesome human needs, sick at heart over the church's reliance on cheap grace, and influenced by the published experiences of the people in the Church of Our Saviour in Washington, D.C.—have identified themselves as "covenanting" congregations. They count as members each year only those who pledge in writing a measure of their money, time, and skills for Christ's ministry in and through their particular congregations. Covenanting is one way of doing stewardship. The congregations which live together in this fashion testify to the soundness of the practice.

Protestant congregations are flabby in defining membership in the *institutional* church. They are more careless than concerned about the people who commit themselves to Christ's care in and through the Christian congregation for which they have oversight. Jesus spoke unequivocally about obedience, self-discipline, the narrow gate, and the cross. If too many church members are relying on cheap grace—and they are—it is because the church is dispensing it, fearful that speaking and doing God's demands will undercut radically the limited economic support now being provided for its institutional life. The world in the church, not the Word, writes the agenda for too many congregations.

Free-Will Offerings

While the use of signed pledges and weekly envelopes reflects free-will giving, we recognize here the thousands of congregations which do not use either pledge cards or weekly envelopes but rely instead on cash gifts placed on the offering plates at *all* services of public worship.

There are many congregations throughout the country, especially small congregations and sectarian fellowships (white as well as black), which cling to this frontier-rural practice from nineteenth-century America. To be sure, all congregations have some members who give in this fashion, but the majority of contributors in main-line Protestant churches in 1976 use the congregation's weekly envelopes, contribute by check, or rely on automatic bank payments. This is true because of denomination-wide teaching *and* the possibility of being checked on by the Internal Revenue Service.

The means which church members employ for giving money for Christ's ministry are not the primary criteria for judging any congregation's stewardship. If, through free-will cash gifts at worship services, the members contribute from love of Christ and concern for their neighbors, and do that deed regularly without constant emotional harangues from the pulpit about money, the Lord is pleased. Free-will (cash) offerings remain one way of doing stewardship in many American churches.

The Stewardship and Finance Committees

Stewardship is the responsibility of the congregation. But the making of budgets, the presentation of the budget, the mechanics of receiving pledges and offerings, and the keeping of financial records is the responsibility of the official board. Most boards delegate these and other specific responsibilities to committees. They appoint committees for (1) parish education, (2) evangelism, (3) stewardship, (4) worship and music, (5) finance, and (6) executive matters. Larger, more widely involved congregations have additional committees (social ministry, social action, social issues, personnel, investments) which reflect the work they are doing. Ordinarily, in these days of shared decision-making, all committees are chaired by members of the official board and staffed with members *from the congregation* as well as from the board.

In May or June (if the congregation's fiscal year ends December 31), the official board asks its committees to examine the work for which they are responsible and project their budget needs for the coming year. These committee estimates, carefully framed, are reviewed by the finance committee in early September. The finance committee in turn constructs the full budget, which it presents in October to the official board, which, in turn, accepts or amends and then approves the full budget. The stewardship committee sees that the services of pledging, pledges-by-mail, or the every-member canvass, together with any literature that is used and the distribution of envelopes for the coming year, are accomplished efficiently. The final budget is approved or amended on the basis of the pledging to reflect real expectations. Integrity should characterize the administration of the parish.

Christian stewardship is motivated and shaped by a personal-communal commitment to God, who creates and sustains, redeems and liberates, enlightens and heartens responsive persons. It depends on God's gracious action *and* man's disciplined response in freedom to God's deed in Christ.